C000088424

100 + TOP TIPS

FOR

SOCIAL MEDIA SUCCESS

Maggie Davies and Sue Smith

Licence Notes

100+ Top Tips for Social Media Success

First published 2016

100+ Top Tips is an imprint of Next Steps Group Ltd.

2 Crossways Business Centre, Kingswood, Aylesbury, HP18 0RA
UK

www.100toptipbooks.com

Print ISBN: 978-0-9570-085-4-0
eBook ISBN: 978-0-9570-085-5-7

A CPI catalogue record for this book is available from the British Library.

Books in this series

BLUE BOOKS FOR PERSONAL DEVELOPMENT

100 + TOP TIPS FOR JOB SEEKERS
ISBN 978-095700-853-3

100 + TOP TIPS FOR DEVELOPING YOUR CAREER
ISBN 978-095700-858-8

100 + TOP TIPS FOR EFFECIVE LEADERSHIP
ISBN 978-0-9934658-6-4

100 + TOP TIPS FOR MANAGING YOUR COACHING NEEDS
ISBN 978-0-9934658-7-1

RED BOOKS FOR IMPROVING YOUR ORGANISATION – SMALL AND LARGE

100 + TOP TIPS FOR SETTING UP AND RUNNING AN
ONLINE BUSINESS
ISBN 978-099346-580-2

100 + TOP TIPS FOR EFFECTIVE SALES MANAGEMENT
ISBN 978-095700-859-5

100 + TOP TIPS FOR SOCIAL MEDIA SUCCESS
ISBN 978-095700-854-0

100 + TOP TIPS FOR SETTING UP YOUR OWN BUSINESS
ISBN 978-099346-585-7

100 + TOP TIPS FOR UNDERSTANDING BUSINESS
FINANCE
ISBN 978-0-9934658-9-5

Books can be purchased from www.100toptipsbooks.com or all good bookshops.

Introduction

Social media is acknowledged as a wonderful opportunity to promote your business, your products, your expertise and your brand to a huge audience. However, social media is not always as easy as it appears and has many potential traps and pitfalls. This is where the contents of this book can help you.

Even if you don't have a business to promote, this book will help to improve your awareness of how social media works. It's definitely beneficial for those whose budget doesn't extend to covering the costs of hiring an agency or Expert.

If you only want to use social media for the social aspect, you will find lots of information on how to go online safely. The book may give you ideas for using your leisure time in ways you have never imagined in the past.

Written in a clear, easily readable style, avoiding a multitude of acronyms and tech speak, it gives you answers to many questions and also suggestions for important decisions regarding your marketing online.

There are a variety of aspects covered. Starting by understanding your brand, through the choices of platform, managing the workload and assessing the results to ensure you get the most out of your online presence.

Maggie and Sue have captured a wealth of useful tips and knowledge from their extensive knowledge and experience in business and personal use. They highlight how social media can be both an excellent promotional tool but also a time-consuming trial. In this book they share practical ways to cut through the background noise and support your success.

Included within the book are names of organisations which provide information and tools on subjects from regulation through to practical advice on all aspects of social media.

To ensure an unbiased and independent view, these organisations have been selected after research or recommendation. The authors and publishers do not have any contractual arrangements with any companies mentioned and do not benefit financially or otherwise from their inclusion.

100 + Top Tips For Social Media Success

Social media is constantly evolving and sites are always adding new services. So, providing some top tips makes this one of those books that will need constant updating – good news to those who buy this book in paperback or eBook format as electronic updates can be freely downloaded from our user's forum.

Please give us your feedback which will help us to keep our content fresh and updated. Contact us, Maggie and Sue, at socialmedia@100toptips.com

Maggie Davies   Sue Smith

Contents

Chapter 1 – Creating Your Brand

Branding is important in everything we do. Often when we think of branding, we think of a product and identify with the thoughts, feelings and expectations we have of it. This is also the case for a company, our experience, its values and association with what that means to us.

You are your own product and need to market yourself in a consistent, professional manner conveying the same story and message, however we communicate with our audience.

Jeff Bezos, the Founder of Amazon, sums this up nicely – *"Brand is what people say about you when you are not in the room"*. Therefore, we need to formulate a strategy to influence what people say about us.

1   What is a Brand?

There are two levels of branding we need to consider depending on the business and the service offered. First, our Company brand, second our personal brand. The two should be very closely linked. Both the company and your values need to be closely aligned. Your company focus should be linked to your own goals.

This symbiosis is a bit like a seesaw, if one side is more heavily weighted than the other, the balance is tipped and you may become known for only one side of the equation. This balancing is important to manage as feedback from customers and clients can often tip in either a positive or negative way. Once defined you need to build, nurture and maintain your brand. Here are some key things to consider about a Brand:

- Your brand is tool that helps people identify with you, not a slogan, logo or recognisable image, these are all marketing tools to convey the message.

- It is what we share, what we say, how we look, how we interact and the message we convey that constitutes our personal brand.

- When our personal brand and our business brand are aligned this becomes our brand identity.

- Our business brand is what our customers relate to; our products, services, company name, impression that they have of us. Often intangible, but it is how a customer relates to your organisation.

- Your brand whether personal or company, can be your greatest asset and you may want to consider trademarks, copyright, or other legal standards to protect your brand. See Chapter 9 for more on legalities and section 5 Trademarks and Logos in this Chapter.

- You may use a particular product name or have designed some software or even want to trademark your own name to protect this valuable commodity, your brand could be that point of difference between you and your closest competitor.

When we consider personal brand and your business brand, we need to consider the following:

What is your brand strategy?

Your personal and company brand strategy should both convey:

- How you can help me, why do I need you?
- Who you are and what is your expertise in this field?
- What you do and why you do it?
- What you offer and how you deliver this?

To help you with this you could carry out the exercise to define your business strategy using a Focus Document, you can find more information in the Learning Zone at www.100toptipsbooks.com.

When building a brand, you also need to consider a strapline.

2 Why do I need a Brand?

Hopefully reading this far has encouraged you to recognise the importance of a Brand not only for your company but for you too. Here are some more reasons why a brand is important:

- A strong, recognisable, and believable brand will allow you to build relationships with your audience, hopefully turning them into loyal customers.

- Clarity and consistency of your message, style and look of your brand will help you to focus on what is important to you and others and help create authenticity. Making you more believable and "real".

- You can convey what makes you different to others, think about your story, why you do what you do as this will be unique and can help you to stand out from the crowd. If people buy into you, they will buy into your company or products.

- Branding helps create a memorable, lasting impression on your consumers.

- Think of a brand you know, we often refer to a product by its brand name rather than what it is.

For example:

> A Hoover/Dyson – it's a vacuum cleaner
> A Kleenex – it's a tissue
> A Biro – it's a pen
> A Band-Aid – it's a plaster
> And the list goes on…….

The way these brands have been marketed, defines the association we have with them. Think about some brand names, what do you associate them with?

What do you want your audience to associate with you and your products or company? Use the exercises in section 10 of this Chapter to help.

3   Defining your Brand

When we define our brand, what we are really doing is strategically positioning who we are, what we do and what we want to be known for, before our customers do this for us.

First, you need to decide what your business will be called and how you will operate. Will you use Ltd status, is it a partnership, charity or are you going to act as a sole trader? There is lots of support on the .Gov website; start your own business, that will guide you through all the different entities and what they involve. So, if you are not sure, start here. When you have chosen the route to operate then:

- Create a unique business name. You want to make sure that no one that offers a similar service to you is using the name you thought of.

- Google search your shortlist. If someone is already using this name, they may own a website or the domain name.

- Once you have decided on the business name, register it at Companies House, purchase the domain name, and set up a company email address ASAP. See Chapter 2.

- Be quick! Often, as soon as you look up a company at Companies House, lots of trawling software will pick up the search terms and if you are not careful someone may purchase the domain to inflate the resale price.

- Be clear on the name, then quickly claim all the associated versions of domain where appropriate, e.g. .com, .co.uk or .global, there are hundreds of domain name extensions so choose those most appropriate for your business. You will find more information in Chapter 4- Website Creation.

- Register the business on all social media sites that you intend to use. This secures the page name and even if you choose not to use it, no one else can. See Chapter 3.

Once you have the business name, then you need to be clear on what you offer:

- Define your unique selling points. What is going to set you apart from your competitors? Is it the superior product or customer service they will receive or maybe the value?

- Think about what makes you different and use this to your benefit. Avoid being all things to everyone as this can devalue your brand, and make your message appear confused or lacking professionalism.

- Conduct market research across multiple platforms. What do your competitors claim to do? How do they share this message? What can you do better than them or offer as a point of difference?

- What is your backstory? Why do you do what you do, why are you passionate about this industry, cause or service? This is often described as our personal USP (unique selling point), as only you have this story to tell.

- Generate a "mission statement" or a headline/strapline for your company. Make it short and snappy, something clear and memorable that clearly links to your business. See section 10 for an exercise to build your own.

This is also the point where you may consider a logo or visuals for your company communication. See section 4. It may be important for you or your company to consider trademarks, copyright or intellectual property rights, we cover more on this in section 5 – Trademarks and Logos.

4   Visuals

Pictures

Visuals can make a huge difference to your audience's response to your content. They are quickly processed by individuals, measured in milliseconds, which is many times faster than text.

HubSpot research states that visual content is 40 times more likely to get shared on social media than any other type of content. They also say that 80% of people will watch a video vs 20% reading the text. And visual content will be remembered by 65% of people almost 3 days later. The importance of good visuals is vital. See Chapter 6 - Content Creation.

Fonts

Fonts, like fashion, rise and fall in their popularity. Certain fonts are indicative of an era – think about art deco, art nouveau or the psychedelic sixties. Be careful of the font you use for your business artwork, your website or blog content or any written promotional material. Some facts for you to consider:

- Over 200,000 fonts exist in the world.

- Typeface refers to different lettering designs.

- Each variation (bold, italicised, underlined) of a typeface is called a font.

As the choice of fonts is so important to websites, you will find the main content within Chapter 4 – Setting up your website.

Colours

The colours you use to project your brand, write content on your website or even the backgrounds for your visuals are all important and can influence reactions from your audience. There are key factors to take into account when choosing your colours for your brand and within all aspects of where you promote your business. For more details see Chapter 4 - Website Creation.

- Emotional responses.

- Colour blindness.

- High or low contrast.

5   Protecting my Brand.

Thinking about what you have to do to create your brand, you need to protect your brand and ultimately your reputation before someone else, to start to trade off your success. This section explores some ways that you can protect your brand and fend off those copycats.

What is Intellectual Property?

Anything that you have created using your mind can be classed as Intellectual Property often known as IP. Any logos you create, materials you write, documents you share, artistic content and so on can be classed as IP.

There are 4 main types of IP:

- Trademarks
- Patents
- Copyright
- Trade Secrets

As these topics fall under legalities, this part of the book is designed to get you to think about what to consider, it is not an exhaustive or legal guide to what you must do.

Please do search for the latest guidance or employ a legal expert to help you explore and identify what is right for you and your business.

What are Trademarks?

Trademarks are usually associated with a product or name, a logo or your strapline. When you register your trademark, you'll be able to:

- Take legal action against anyone who uses your brand without your permission, including counterfeiters.

- Put the ® symbol next to your brand - to show that it's yours and warn others against using it.

- Sell and license your brand.

There are rules with what you can and can't trademark. Again the .Gov website will explain the most recent of these but in general here are some guidelines. Your trademark must be unique. It can include:

- Words
- Sounds
- Logos
- Colours
- A combination of any of these

Your trademark cannot:

- Be offensive, e.g. contain swear words or pornography.

- Describe the goods or services it will relate to, for example the word 'cotton' cannot be a trademark for a cotton textile company.

- Be misleading, for example use the word 'organic' for goods that are not organic.

- Be a 3-dimensional shape associated with your trademark, for example the shape of an egg for eggs.

- Be too common and non-distinctive, for example be a simple statement like "we lead the way".

- Look too similar to state symbols like flags or hallmarks, based on World Intellectual Property Organisation guidelines.

Before you start the process of trademarking, check the Trademarks data base to make sure that no one else has already trade marked the areas you are considering.

If you do find something similar to yours, you can approach the existing holder for a "letter of consent". This may take time and be a costly process so think about any alternatives before you embark on this process.

You might consider registering a trademark. This registration can be done via the .gov website and will guide you through the process in a step-by-step way.

The whole process can take around 4 months, if no one opposes your application, and lasts for 10 years. So, make sure you set a reminder to renew!

How can Patents help?

"A patent is the granting of a property right by a sovereign authority to an inventor. A patent provides the inventor exclusive rights to the patented process, design, or invention for a certain period in exchange for a complete disclosure of the invention."

- Patents are usually used when creating a new product or process that has never been marketed before.

- If you have an invention that you feel you want to patent, keep it under wraps until you have filed the application on the UK Intellectual Property Office (IPO).

You will find many web resources to help you should you need to patent anything, one good resource is the British Library website. This is a great guide for business start-up and gives thorough guidance to all things business.

What about Copyright?

Here is a definition taken from Wikipedia:

"A copyright is a type of intellectual property that gives its owner the exclusive right to copy and distribute a creative work, usually for a limited time. The creative work may be in a literary, artistic, educational, or musical form."

- So, copyright protects the work you create from being used without your permission.

- In the UK there is no register of copyright, you automatically get copyright protection and can use the copyright symbol (©), your name and the year of creation to express this explicitly to others.

Copyright can be a key process to explore, get help from the .Gov website but do engage with a legal professional for the best advice and how to protect yourself further. See Chapter 5 – Blogs, Vlogs and Podcasts, Topic 9 – Copyright and Legalities.

What are Trade Secrets?

The Trade Secrets Act was bought about to protect the confidential exchange of information between two companies or partners. It relates to a piece of information which is treated as confidential by its owner and has value.

This may be information you share at a meeting, advice you have provided, an idea that you share with a customer. You have to show that you have taken steps to keep information a secret, not shared this publicly previously or broadcast the information in any way. Some simple steps you can take include:

- Create and sign a Confidentially Agreement before any exchanges of information. Often referred to as Non-Disclosure Agreements (NDAs).

- If you employ others, make sure that this NDA is written into employment contracts.

- Mark documents as "Private and Confidential" and use disclaimers at the end of emails stating for the addressee's attention only and not for onward distribution.

- Make sure all physical and electronic filing systems are always secured.

- Restrict access to critical information to key employees only.

You may want to research this further, especially if you are bringing a new product, process, or invention to the market and need to canvass support from others. Seek legal advice if appropriate, this section of the book is designed simply to raise awareness to these issues.

6   Developing your Message

Earlier in this chapter we looked at what is a brand and how to start your brand strategy. Now we need to bring this together to start to communicate this clearly and objectively to our target market.

There are 4 stages to communicating your brand:

- Define your strategy and stick to it. We looked at this in earlier sections and if you are still yet to define who your customers are, or what you are going to offer, please use the exercises in section 10 of this chapter.

- Clearly identify what your point of difference is and make sure this is communicated at all opportunities.

- Think about your values, your pillars of success, what you want to be known for or as, make sure you think about your message and does it relay this to your audience.

- Communicate across all channels in a consistent, focused way that supports your brand and appeals to your target market.

When we think of getting our message out there, we have many options and ways we can do this.

You will find more information in Chapter 6 – Content Creation, but you should strongly consider:

- Blogs, vlogs, podcasts, and videos – See Chapter 5

- Social Media channels – See Chapter 3 for more details

- Your website – Creation and content, Chapter 4

- Networking – Chapter 7

The key to strong branding is consistency of message. It can be time consuming to create content, you may want to look for existing content to share or comment on.

- Define what topics are going to be useful to your audience. Pick up to 5 key areas to start with, gather content that you feel is relevant, informative, useful.

- Note these down as your "hot topics" that you will focus on to find and share content on. You may even progress to writing your own.

- Create a spreadsheet of websites, weblinks, information sources that you can refer to.

- Set up a search on a trawling site such as Google Alerts (free to use) to find content related to topics of interest can be helpful.

- Make sure you are sharing frequently as many posts and articles can be time dependant and you want to show that you are keeping up with industry and sector innovation and change.

- Use scheduling sites and tools within those social media channels you choose to pre-load content and share at a pre-determined date and time.

- Research the best times to post on each channel, be active when your target market is using the sites.

You can "piggyback" on other people's posts and articles, and you can follow most people on their social media pages and receive their updates in your feeds and threads. Look for industry thought leaders, respected operators in your field, anyone of interest to you or your audience.

- Do an internet search on the top influencers on various social channels, for your areas of interest. Follow them and interact with them via their posts and articles.

- Adding comments on platforms, not simply liking, or hitting the share button, not just retweeting but quote tweeting on twitter for example, will raise the number of views your interactions get.

- You can use the "@" to mention someone, they are notified that you have mentioned them and if they respond all their followers will see and may take an interest in what you have to say.

Create your own content and publish on any sites you can.

- Some sites, like LinkedIn, will allow you to write articles and hold them until you are ready to publish them, you add in images, web sources, direct to other social media sites or webpages, all by using the online simple author tools.

- The hardest part with content creation is the writing. It often takes longer than you anticipated to write something you are happy to share. Make sure you have enough time to do this, and enough content to share.

- If readers have enjoyed your content, they will be looking for more! Make sure you have at least 6 articles worth of content written before you publish so that you have ready-made releases, which allow you time to write some more

- Remember posts can be fun as well as informative, you may have an office mascot who travels or a feature on pets in the team. This may add a little more light-hearted personality into your posts.

You may have lots of data and reports of interest:

- Repurpose content and activities, you may have some analytics that you have presented in an infographic or presentation, is this useful to share?

- Turn a physical brochure into a e-brochure, post this on your website or social channels.

Your target market needs to know who you are, what you do, where to find you and how to get in touch. You could through advertising in the trade press, local or national news, radio, posters, direct mail shots/flyers, direct emails, and your website and maybe in partnership with associated organisations. All of these different sources will help you to reach your audience.

Your message, using flyers and business cards, email signatures etc. requires careful thought and administration. Consistency is key, the colours, logo, strapline and any other business branding you use should appear on all communications.

- Set your branding guidelines for all that will create or distribute content on behalf of you or your company.

- Consider the font style, size, colour combinations, logo size, positioning on the page and make sure everyone has these guidelines and sticks to them (see more in Chapter 4 for help with visuals and accessibility).

- Define the style of writing or content you want to be associated with. Make sure all who need to be briefed are on what is or is not appropriate content for distribution.

- Make sure that you have a Social Media Policy for employees in place. Can they promote other companies? Comment on company business or competitor products or services? Write this into any employment contracts.

- Provide a template for email signatures, including your logo and links to other social media channels. Make it easy for colleagues to be consistent.

- You might even use this signature to promote events or content releases with a "coming soon" campaign.

The frequency of posts can also affect your brand. Too many posts and articles may swamp your audience and leave them feeling bombarded with your activity.

To help you manage this you could:

- Create a marketing diary, add in any notable events that you want to include as areas of focus, this may be seasons, festivals, event weeks, or themes, i.e. National Book Week etc. These can be loosely associated with your business, you might start a discussion about the most influential book you have read and why during National Book Week.

- Use a teaser campaign, so your audience knows what is coming and when to look out for content. There is no point going "live" on any channel (Facebook, LinkedIn etc) if people are not aware of this.

- Assign the marketing activity to a team member if you have the resources to allow this.

If writing your own content becomes too time consuming, or maybe you don't have the confidence at the start, freelancers could help. There are a number of freelancer sites available peopleperhour.com, upwork.com, guru.com, worksome.com, fiverr.com, truelancer.com, reedsey.com.

7   Your Target Market

To reach your target market you need to identify who they are, what they do, where they use social media, etc. Ask yourself:

What is the demographic of your target market?

- What is the age range of your chosen audience?

- What gender are they?

- What location do they live in?

- What time zone if international?

What do they do?

- What do they do for a living?

- What industry or sector do they work in?

- What is their spending power? Critical for high end products or service.

- What are their interests? Sport for example, what areas of social media might be good to place your posts and interactions?

What Stage of Life are they at?

- New Parents?
- Retired / semi-retired / planning retirement?
- Students, University or College?
- Apprentices?
- Teens?

Who has the Buying Power?

- Is it the individual, their Parents?
- Is it the business? What size of business are you looking to attract?
- Who are the decision makers in that business? Are you targeting the right level of role?

The answers to these four simple questions can then be used to identify what platforms they are likely to use, what are the best times to post, and if national or local groups would be better for you.

Find the specific sites used by your target organisation or individuals – LinkedIn, Facebook, Twitter etc. and follow and like their pages. Start to make a connection with them.

- Make sure you are looking for your audience in the right place. Access demographic information and usage statistics to ensure the sites you are using are correct for your offering.
- Download your contacts from LinkedIn, this can help to identify your "hot" network, those that you know well, or if you download this into excel you can apply filters to identify target companies, sectors or job titles.
- Prepare who you will communicate with, when you will do this, and how.

What media is best for promoting your offering?

- Don't think you have to use every media option out there – choose what is right for you and your offering.
- Check which sites your competition uses.
- Will you get a better response to your offering on Facebook or Twitter?
- If you are promoting yourself perhaps LinkedIn would be the best option.

When you start to interact on social media, you need to know you are reaching the right audience. You can view the latest demographics from Khoros.com.

These are the 4 main sites, but a search for demographics for your chosen platform will give you similar statistics as will some of the sites themselves.

The statistics have shown that there is no real difference in gender use of these sites, and more affluent people tend to use social media more, the only odd one here is Facebook, where income does not really affect the rate of use.

In summary, do your research, and make sure that you are talking to the right people in the right space for you.

- Look where your competitors have a presence, especially those looking to attract the same audience. Search their sites, look at the platforms they feature on and learn from those using social media well.

- Use the inbuilt analytics tools on the social media sites, you may have to pay for this data. Knowing who is looking at your posts, interacting and spending time on your website or social channels is valuable information.

- You could consider if the location of your target audience is regionally specific? If so, using regional or location driven groups would be preferable to general posts to a national audience or vice versa.

- What stage of life is your target market? You may not be in this demographic yourself so surveying your target market, using panel meetings or discussion groups might help to identify the right platforms to use.

- Remember new social sites are constantly evolving. Sites for University students, local communities, sites to chat on and so on all appear and disappear just as quickly. Canvass opinion, stay in touch with the market and you will be able to ensure that you reach your intended target.

8   How to be Authentic.

Authenticity is what makes us believable and credible. It helps our target market to understand clearly who we are, what we stand for, what we do or believe in, and to see us as a trusted partner.

- Be consistent. The headshot photo we use, the background banner, our company logo, the look and feel of the pages all need to be the same consistent image.

- Image is not only visuals, but also the style that we use to write. This is equally important. Your consistent style makes you more connected to the reader.

Secondly:

- Be HUMAN, tell people what you are passionate about, what is important to you. Perhaps you or your company sponsor a good cause or have strong links to the community. Research shows that customers relate better to businesses they can relate to.

- Let people know your history or story. Maybe write a feature or article on your journey so far. What you did in the past, what you loved about it, what has driven you to where you are today? If appropriate, you may add something a little more personal.

- Show people what it is like within your company. Maybe a "Day In The Life Of" feature.

Thirdly:

- Share success! Get reviews, publish feedback, get people talking about your business and interact with them and share their recommendations, comments and so on.

- Managing your reputation is key. Whilst you are seeking the good points, you also need to look for and manage the bad.

- Make sure you have a process in place for managing complaints and your team are aware of this.

- Put a search on your company name for mentions on social media sites, Google alerts or monitoring sites. Respond to complaints swiftly, but take the discussion offline, and ask the customer to post an update once successfully resolved.

Lastly:

- Get your customers not only to review you, but also invite them to generate content, this is known as user generated content or "UGC".

- UGC could include videos of your product in use, a story, review and so on.

- Encourage the use of #'s to get a broader view of the UGC. Start a #campaign. Think of a creative title, encourage users to share using the # across multiple platforms.

- Often you can mediate content before it is publicly shared, so check out how to mediate posts in groups of discussion boards you administer.

9   How to get your brand noticed.

Now you have defined your brand, created content, found our audience and created associated marketing plans, you need to get your brand out there and make it searchable.

You can pay any site to be featured. This could be on Facebook Ads, page promotions, affiliate marketing and so on. If your budget allows this could also be worth exploring. Targeted ads for example can be sent to a certain demographic, those interested in certain content, or associated search terms.

A lot of how we can boost our rankings on search sites is to do with search engine optimisation or SEO. So, if you are looking to get on the first few pages of Google, Yahoo, Bing and other search sites we need to think about how SEO works and what we can manipulate to increase our visibility.

There is lots of information which relates to websites in Chapter 4- Your Website.

- You could send out a post encouraging people not to miss your posts with the instructions on how to do this. Simply hovering over the "like" button and choosing "see first" or "get notifications" will allow your post to appear at the top of your fans' threads.

- To do this people need to like your page first so encourage them to do this. Maybe a promotional offer, some insights you can give, "Like my page to receive…"

- You could turn this into an instructional video, make one for each of the platforms you use. Video is often favoured on sites and improves SEO, the algorithm shows people spend longer watching video.

- Respond quickly to people sharing or commenting on posts on any sites. Being responsive and spending time on the sites also influences the algorithm.

- Use # and "mention" @ on social media sites and encourage your network to do this too. They may not be natural users of the platform and may not realise if they include your business name as a mention that this will help you or if they use a # the content will be seen more widely.

- You may need to be selective with who you ask to do this and may favour the less formal sites out there as the user population may be more attuned to this type of activity.

- On LinkedIn try the #feature in posts and articles, mentions. You can also use features such as "talks about" to show people what you are associated with. Remember you can also share video on this site too.

- Cross promote content, use scheduling tools to promote the same content on different platforms at different times, or link your LinkedIn and Twitter feeds together. You can do this in your privacy controls.

- Keep up to date with new features on social media sites. Run regular searches for "what's new on...." follow the tutorials and see if these features would benefit you.

- Use groups on social sites, these are often ready-made networks to tap into, but be careful not to direct sell, you may be excluded from the group!

In general, we need to include as many key words as we can on our social media pages. Remember many new clients will not be searching for your business name, they will be searching for services, expertise, qualifications and so on.

Make sure these are included in profiles, bios, the about section of your website, but make sure you are aware of what your audience will look for.

- Conduct some market research. You could do this with a poll on social media sites to canvas opinion and gain interaction.

- Ask questions like what would you search on to find X? Use the most popular responses to double check you are including these.

- Become a customer! Search for what you want and see who comes up at the top of the search results.

- You can narrow down searches by using Boolean Search Language. This allows you to insert words or phrases such as AND, OR, NOT to limit, broaden and define the search results. This is detailed in Chapter 4.

10 Exercises to help and a checklist

Using a "Focus" document to clearly and concisely describe how clients/customers will benefit from your services. See the Learning Zone at www.100toptipsbooks.com.

A Focus document - which should not be larger than one page - has a number of practical uses.

- It helps define your brand.
- An introductory document to send to a prospective client before a meeting.
- A discussion document with networking contacts.
- A framework for a PowerPoint presentation.
- The core content for a web site.

Your Checklist of Activity

Action – Have you?	Complete	What will help?
Defined your company name?		
Registered the Domain Name?		
Created a business email?		
Completed a focus document?		
Designed a logo?		
Created a strapline or mission statement?		
Set up social media accounts with your or your business name?		
Built your profile/bios and business pages on these sites?		
Identified your "hot topics" that		

you will follow and share?		
Identified your "influencers" / thought leaders to follow?		
Your own content written in to share?		
Listed resources to refer to for content?		
Decided frequency of sharing?		
Using a content management site to schedule posts?		

Defining your Brand

We need to identify what makes us different, what is our USP or Unique Selling Point. This exercise is designed to help you to explore these factors.

What will you offer?	How is this different to my competitors?	Why are you best at this?
Online coaching and training services	Many offer face to face only I will offer virtual, and at more flexible times	Having run global training and coaching sessions on Zoom, Teams, and many other platforms we offer a professional service using the features of these sites to allow a personal experience

		likened to a live event
Individual and group sessions	*Many only offer group sessions and limit numbers*	*Have the flexibility to design bespoke solutions for your needs not one solution fits all approach*
Fill in yours here		

This exercise may help you to develop your "elevator pitch" or that 60 second intro of who you are and what you do.

Try this exercise for both introducing yourself and your business.

Your Elevator Pitch

Here are some questions to help you develop your elevator pitch.

Remember this is a quick 60 second intro to you and what you offer.

1 – What is your goal for this pitch?

Like everything we need to understand why we are doing something, what is our objective for this activity. An elevator pitch is no different.

- Do you want to let people know about your or your business?
- A product or a service?
- Why are you building this pitch?

2 – What do they need to know about you or your offer?

- Who are you? What are you?
- What do you do or specialise in?

3 – Why choose you?

- What are you a specialist in?

- What is your unique selling point or USP?

- What makes you better than the rest?

4 – What is your background?

- What is important to summarise about your career or background?

- This may well relate to or have been covered in point 3, so no need to repeat if that is the case.

- Do you have any relevant qualifications?

Answer these questions then practice your delivery. You may want to do this a few times, you may want to mix up the order of delivery. Remember being authentic is using your own style. So, talk about this in a natural spontaneous style, do not simply learn this to allow you to repeat in a parrot fashion! A good elevator pitch is telling a quick but engaging story, these questions are just a guide to what you may include, but think about what is important to your customer and what they need to hear from you too.

Your Mission Statement/Strapline

In this exercise think of a punchy headline that you can use on all marketing materials.

Reflect on what other organisations have used, I have included some big corporates here that you might recognise but do think about this for your size of business and what makes you different.

British Airways – "To Fly to Serve"

Tesco – "Every Little Helps"

Nike – "Just Do It"

Apple – "Think Different"

Loreal – "Because your Worth It"

Think about your five words exercise, can you incorporate any of this into your strapline?

Joe Bloggs Computing – "Business Focused, User Friendly Solutions"

Sally Jones Hair Design – "Creative, Beautiful, Affordable"

Chapter 2 – Essential Preparation

1 Administration

You need to ensure that you have adequate supplies of any promotional materials you are going to use, but balance this with the likelihood of them becoming dated or any details or offers changing. You also need to investigate formal administration systems to manage invoicing etc.

- Keep all your social media, website and business information secure along with the passwords and access requirements.

- Investigate QR codes with regard to the speedy capture of your information. QR codes can be generated for free, do not expire and are easy to generate and use.

- Reduce hard copy materials and try to print/produce only enough needed for a particular campaign.

- If you are going to print on demand and do this yourself the quality of the materials produced need to reflect your brand professionally.

- Ensure all your contact details are listed, including website and social media address.

- Sending invoices, estimates, letters via email is far more cost effective than hard copy and postage. Make sure that you have files set up in your email to make the tracking and monitoring of these documents easier.

You could purchase an online accountancy package to create your invoices, help you to track your expenses and also register payment from customers and clients.

- If you are going to use media such as Groupon to promote special offers make sure that you have enough stock or can fulfil all demand, if not this could damage your reputation. You will be able to discuss the likely take up of offers when negotiating rates with Groupon directly.

2 Choosing the right social media platforms

As covered in Chapter 1 Branding section, most people use a selection of social media but often for different reasons. You don't need to use every platform, it would be time consuming and potentially have a negative impact on your brand. To make your selection you need to consider your audience, your offering, the competition and your marketing goals.

- Investigate what platform your customers use for your type of product. If your competition is already there, it's probably because it's profitable for them.

- Some sites are much more visuals based like Instagram, Pinterest, YouTube and TikTok, others lean more towards the written word. All of them have their own style and communication methods.

- Blogs, vlogs and podcasts are all considered to be social media elements and can be used as stand-alone methods of communication or accessed from a more usual platform, like Facebook or Instagram.

- Keep your brand consistent but you may have to adapt and tailor your content when you present it on the various sites.

- Social media will use your time, consider how many hours you will allocate to updating before you commit to taking on too many sites.

3   Researching the competition

There are many options to search out your competition. You want to find out who they are, where they are, what they offer and how much they charge. Some details will be public however don't be scared of doing your own customer research.

- Use LinkedIn, Facebook, Instagram etc to search by individual name – see what they say about themselves.

- Look at company pages on various sites to see what services they are offering and how they position themselves to potential and existing customers/clients.

- Carry out searches on the platforms your competition use using your key words or skills, assess the results. View others' profiles to see how they have positioned themselves and why they are appearing on your results.

- Make a general "Google" search for your type of business in your geographic area to find your competition, you may then decide to follow these companies on Twitter or similar.

4   Communication methods and regularity

However you decide to communicate to your customers and potential market you need to keep your delivery in line with expectation. The regularity of updates needs to be manageable for your business and the content should reflect your brand as well as the message to want to share.

- Established social network sites like Facebook, Twitter, LinkedIn, Instagram give you an easily accessible customer base quickly.

- Blogs and Vlogs are great to share information and prompt discussion. TikTok has grown massively across the globe and can assist in promoting diverse businesses.

- Gain feedback from sites like TripAdvisor or set up contests and requests for reactions on standard social media sites.

- Remember to use hashtags, for example #smallbusiness, #handmade, #supportsmallbusiness.

- Email marketing is making a comeback, it needs to be personalised and pertinent for people to react positively. Use some of the professional organisations to manage your campaign. Mailchimp offers a free start to get on board and if it proves of benefit you can get onto a contract basis.

- Consider using scheduling sites such as Hootsuite or Blogger to help send out posts and updates with preloaded times to multiple platforms at once.

Your email address depicts your brand every time someone sees it or uses it. It's important to consider the content of the address and how it is formatted.

- Aim for a consistent branding, if you can obtain the domain name for your business and secure an email address "@domain" this looks more professional and serious than a free email address.

- If you don't yet have a website, you can purchase the domain name and utilise this for emails until your website is built, or ongoing dependent upon your line of work.

- Choose sensible business-like email addresses, they could be separated by function –"sales@domain", "admin@domain".

- Set up a separate email address for your personal emails and keep your contacts apart for ease of communication.

5 Website preparation

There are different elements to preparing an effective website. Your site may be delivered by a design company, friends or family or perhaps yourself. Regardless of who is going to create your site you are responsible for the content and its layout.

Good preparation is vital to ensure your site works for you and not against you.

- Prepare a straw man prior to going live. List key areas of interest for your target audience and capture content to support topics.

- It is a legal requirement that your site should be accessible to all, or as many people as technically possible. Should you make an error out of ignorance, and it is highlighted to you, it is important to rectify this as soon as possible. Apart from the legal impact it could also affect your organisation.

- There are accessibility guidelines available which will detail advice for fonts, colours, contrast, gadgets, images etc.

- Ensure the written and visual content represents your brand throughout the site.

More details can be found in Chapter 4-Website Creation.

6 Selecting suppliers or production methods

You do not need to be an expert to be able to produce a professional presentation of your business online.

- Dependent upon your budget you could use a specialised agency to create all aspects of your online presence. If you do, ensure you understand exactly what you need them to do for you and, crucially, understand the costs of both production and ongoing support.

- Instead of a full agency you could also consider a professionally produced logo or letterhead, weigh up the costs for your business. There are many sources of expertise guru.com, peopleperhour.com, fiverr.com, truelancer.com are some to investigate.

- Before you use an agency or freelancer, do your research on their past catalogue of work. Ask yourself if their work is of the calibre and style you are looking for. Cheapest is often not the best value in the end.

- If you are looking for logos or visuals, check if they have been used before, are they under copyright, will you have to pay to use them exclusively.

7 Equipment

Equipment can be one of the biggest purchases a small business can make. Even if you are a sole trader offering consultancy you will still need a phone and a laptop to operate.

Equipment and technology are updating constantly, new operating systems, Apps, ways that your customer is going to want to interact with you. You need to ensure that you are accessible, professional, and responsive at all times.

Every business will need different equipment and possibly a different scale of use.

With regard to utilising the social media elements of running your operation here are the basics you really need to have:

- A Computer. Desktop or Laptop your choice, but it needs to have the latest software and operating systems to ensure you can access all the features on your social sites. You need sufficient RAM, 32GB is a good start. Cloud storage comes free with Microsoft and Apple business packages. Storage, 250GB to start and a good sized external drive for fail safe storage, to allow you to work offline in emergencies.

- A Smart Phone. Make, model is up to you, but consider what you will be using it for.

- Internet access. This is a MUST and you need to research the best provider in your area. Not just on cost but on reliability, speed and capacity.

- Space to work and meet clients. You could hire office space by the day or the hour to meet. You will find flexible office space via companies such as WeWork, Regus. Consider your brand when identifying how and where you will work. Remember the image you are looking to create.

- There are many shared space offices that more of an open plan, hot desk function. These are reasonable in price, and you can collaborate with others and interact. This could be very helpful if others in your industry are in this space to keep up to date and build networks.

- Filing systems and storage. You will need a lockable storage system if you keep hard copy documents with client details, see the data protection section on the .Gov website for up-to-date information on what you need to do to comply.

- General office supplies, chair, desk, stationary etc.

Software

Depending on your business you may need to use specialist software programmes to help with your general management, business automation, accounting, order processing, or data storage. There may be other areas you also need to consider which are specific to your business.

When exploring the software you need, consider the following:

- What do you need the Software to do?

- What platforms of operating systems does it need to be compatible with?

- What security does it offer?

- What can you afford to pay?

- Is there a regulatory / industry standard that you need to meet?

Before you start to engage with providers make sure you have thought about and answered the questions above. Then:

- Research the market, who is providing what you need?

- Talk to your network, what can they recommend?

- Approach the suppliers of the Software, ask for a demonstration based on your needs.

- See if you can negotiate a free trial period, make sure it is right for you and your business.

Often suppliers will sell you a package, you need to understand what is included in that package and to ask questions such as:

- What user support do you provide and how can this be accessed?

- Do you provide an emergency support line? Is this phone or internet chat based?

- How frequently is the software upgraded, and are these updates included in the package?

- Can the programme be modified for your needs (if required)?

- Is there a manual available for this product?

- Do they provide training?

For social media specific software, you might want to investigate programmes that help to:

- Automate posts across various platforms.

- Track success and provide meaningful statistics.

- Allow collaboration of users to post and share under one company.

- Consider sites such as Hootsuite, Buffer, Sprout social as a starting point then look for any other tools that suit your business and budget. Some of these may be free.

You might also include in this section any tools that will help you to share and collaborate with your teams.

- You could look at utilising Microsoft Teams, Zoom, Google Docs and other tools to allow document sharing, live meetings and conferences. All of these tools will work on a mobile device or tablet, so you are able to keep in touch and keep working even away from the office.

8   Business cards and hard copy

Business cards are still useful in today's world. The use of a QR code which contains all your information will allow customers and contacts to capture your details direct to their phone.

- Make sure your business card contains all your key information.

- Business name, your name, a generic job or company descriptor.

- Your contact details – email, mobile/landline, website and social media, plus address if appropriate.

- Social media and networking sites pertinent to your business – LinkedIn, Facebook, Twitter, Instagram, Pinterest etc.

- Remember the impact of colour and design. Add a logo and/or tag line.

- It's important that your card (and your brand in general) clearly identifies your product or service. A card covered in flowers could be either a gardener or a florist dependent upon the representation of the flowers.

- If you intend to hand your card out, consider the size, shape and quality before production.

- There are many sites out there who create business cards, try Moo, Vistaprint and Instaprint online for ideas.

Like business cards, other hard copy e.g. letters, flyers and invoices need the basics, plus some specifics.

Letters – company name, address, email, contact numbers, website and brand logo, plus registration and VAT number if appropriate.

Flyer – company name, contact information brand logo, catchy headline, eye catching visuals and special offers like coupon codes, discounts, sale details, and other relevant information like name of the venue (if there's an event), follow us on...

Invoices – title of Invoice, unique invoice number, company name, address, email, contact numbers, website and brand logo, plus registration and VAT number if appropriate. Customer name and address, description of goods/services, date of supply, date of invoice and the amount of the individual goods or services to be paid, the due date and how to pay.

9 Keywords and written content

Keywords are the words or phrases that you use which your target market will be looking for. They are used on your social media, website, emails and any written content and consistency is important. At this point, collect as many keywords as you can to use when you are preparing your content. For more detailed information go to Chapter 4 – Setting up your Website, Topic 7 – Search engines and Keywords.

Key areas to focus on are and the words to use are:

- Likely to be used by your customers.

- Those used by your competitors.

- Words specific to your business type.

- Acronyms specific to your business type.

Remember that Search Engine Optimisation (SEO) uses keywords and phrases to take customers to relevant content. The better the match the higher up the search results your site may appear.

10 Legal requirements and information

Data protection responsibilities come when you capture people's details if they register on your site and you send them updates or email newsletters. Make sure you are aware of what you need to do and how you should manage the information keeping security at the forefront.

- The Data Protection Act 2018 is the UK's implementation of the General Data Protection Regulation (GDPR). Everyone responsible for using personal data has to follow strict rules called "data protection principles". This gives consumers control over their personal data and online businesses must ask for explicit consent before processing customers' data. Taking this into account you need to be clear about how their data is used and they have the right of access and can request for it to be removed. For more details see www.gov.uk/data-protection

- If you plan to send out email newsletters, you can only mail to private email addresses if you have their express consent and you are obliged to give your recipient a way of unsubscribing. You can ask them to give you a reason for opting out and use this information to improve how you manage your communication.

- Research what your competitor's detail on their websites with regard to Disclaimers and Terms and Conditions.

- There are websites where you can get legal document templates for free. Think about whether you are comfortable relying on a free service.

- There are also sites available where you can purchase legal document templates for a nominal sum for example compactlaw.co.uk.

- Understand how copyright laws work for your industry. Remember, just because you can copy and paste content from a website doesn't mean that you should do it.

- Privacy and Electronic Communications (EC Directive) Regulations 2003 states about informing your customers of the use of cookies and how they are being used.

- All content and images that you use should be free from copyright.

- The Electronic Commerce (EC Directive) Regulations 2002 contains information as to how you communicate with your customer. What you need to display, order details and confirmations and managing your email audit trail.

- The Consumer Protection (Distance Selling) Regulations 2000 concerns B2C (Business to Consumer) protecting the rights of customers. It includes information about postage and packaging costs, cancellations and returns, plus clarity around the products or services, pricing and VAT.

Chapter 3 - Using Social Media Sites

1 Why Use Social Media?

Social media is flourishing with many established and up and coming sites to choose from so you will need to make your choice on the platforms to invest time in dependent upon your own needs.

Using these sites will allow your customers instant access to you and provides you with an efficient marketing and communication tool. When used well these tools can help you to grow and develop your business and communicate your personal brand to a wide, potentially global, audience.

You can use social media to help you find new contacts, to promote your business or services and to approach others. It will also help you to market yourself directly to those you have identified and create a professional online image that you control.

Here are some ways to consider using social media sites:

- To advertise and market your services, speaking directly to your target audience.

- As a free communication tool. Replying to messages, enquiries directly via the platforms in a timely manner. Show your customers you quick to react and keen to interact.

- To research the public's opinions, first-hand, about companies, suppliers, productions, trends etc.

- To maintain and expand your professional networks, increase your client base.

- Track or trace a company name or mention. Ensuring you are aware of what others are saying about you or your competitors.

- Use tools such as Polls to gain your professional audience's opinion within networking groups.

- To help you get found by your audience and help you find them as the traditional ways of advertising are now going online and far more interactive than just an advert in a publication.

- Simply engage with your customers, share useful content, reinforce your brand, stand out as an expert and the list goes on...

So, what sites might you use and why?

LinkedIn

LinkedIn is a professional online networking site that allows you to keep in touch with key contacts, customers and like-minded professionals.

- You create an online image or brand that you wish to be known by and can use this to promote your services or offer to your target market.

Facebook

- Facebook is a great way to keep in touch with your target market. You can set up company pages on Facebook and promote offers, services and new products to your followers and others who may search for you. They also have Facebook Marketplace which allows you to sell direct.

Sharing sites

- Pinterest, Instagram, Snapchat, and YouTube amongst others are also very useful to share images and video clip to your target audience.

- These visual interactions often help to build valuable rapport and relationships by bringing you or your business to life.

2   How can I use LinkedIn?

What is it used for?

LinkedIn is primarily seen as a business-to-business marketing tool. If you are targeting other companies to supply products, services, or information this is a good choice of platform or you.

LinkedIn has a global reach, so you can reach out, connect, communicate and showcase your offer internationally.

LinkedIn allows you to build a number of pages to help you deliver your message of who you are, what you do or specialise in, what services you offer and also create a free company page, so if you prefer to promote your organisation rather than you, the platform allows you to do this for free.

LinkedIn is possibly the main site (other than a well-designed website) that you will share the most information, due to the nature of how it is constructed.

In this section we will look at how to build a great profile page, using the information you created in Chapter 1. This will help to ensure you have a clear, consistent message across all media.

You can access LinkedIn on a laptop or tablet, or by the App on a device. I would recommend setting up your profile and exploring the site using the full web version until you are confident in its use. The App is great for keeping up to date, responding to messages and researching others when you are on the move. Here is how to join the site:

- Go to LinkedIn, click on "Join". The site will ask you for your name, email address and a password of your choice. Once you have completed this it will then ask you to confirm your email address so it knows you are a genuine person.

- Fill in your current or most recent employer, use your company name here, we will cover how to add a logo and build a company page later.

- Once you have completed these initial steps you can now build your profile page. Under the "ME" menu at the top of the page, just click on "edit profile". This is also where you can find the Help guide. To add any content to your profile, just look for the little stylus pencil (edit) or select "Add Section" from the top of the page.

To develop your profile and make sure that you are giving a great impression to your potential target market we would encourage you to:

- Add a professional photo, a picture of how you want to be recognised in a professional context. Use a clear head shot, business dress, with a plain background so people can clearly recognise you and you create the right first impression.

- Use a photo of you "how you would appear". If you are a Construction Site Consultant a photo of you in a hard hat and outdoor jacket would be fine, if you are a Non-Exec Director a photo of you in a more formal guise would be the way forward.

- Use the background banner. This space can help you to reinforce your area of expertise, align you to an industry of sector, or even promote your business with your logo (if you have one) and branding in the background. Try Pixabay and Canva, search by category for suitable images.

- Add qualifications as part of your surname field to showcase relevant qualifications or licences to be instantly credible to your target market. Also add these into the relevant sections of your profile, but these are not immediately seen.

- Make sure your headline reflects what you do, Director at JJB Ltd does not really capture the imagination. Think about what you do, what you specialise in, what are you offering, you have 220 characters to use in this space so use them wisely!

- Fill in your contact details, add in website links if appropriate. You can make your mobile number and email address visible to all LinkedIn members if you are comfortable to share this. You can do this in your privacy controls which you can access under "Me" in the top right corner. Or use the Help function to search who can see my contact details.

- Your "About" section should be about you and what you offer. Again, refer to Chapter 1, Building your Brand and the exercise included there to capture the key points you want to cover. Always write this in the first person, as if you are talking to your audience, but not in the room!

- Add in your Experience, focus on the roles you have held in the past that are most relevant. For most people this will be anything within the last 15 years, anything prior to that is only helpful if it adds value to your offer.

- Think about adding in key achievements, align this to the branding exercise in Chapter 1. What skills are you offering? What are the key elements that support what you offer now in terms of experience, level of operation, specialist areas?

- Add in your Education, most relevant and highest levels. Omit dates if they date you or your qualification, only include dates where they are helpful.

- You can also add in Licences and certifications, honours and awards and other key areas that you choose to.

- Add up to 50 skills, think about how you want to be seen and what you want to be known for. i.e., you might be great at administration, but I am looking to procure your services for strategy development and risk mitigation!

- LinkedIn has several security and privacy controls hidden away. You can generally find these under the Settings function which is under the "ME" area in the top right corner. Hover on this and you should see a drop-down box, choose "privacy and settings" to access your options and controls.

- Please note if you are adding content to your existing profile and have a network in place, LinkedIn will send updates to your networks' feeds to highlight the content you have just added. To stop this, you need to switch off your network updates. LinkedIn will show you at the top of each screen where you add content a toggle switch which will say "yes" to notifying your network. Simply move this to "no" before you save your additions as this will prevent a notification being sent. You are now ready to start making connections!

- You can use the "Contacts" section for suggestions of people you may know, or use the search bar to find people by name, job title, company or skill set on either the full desktop version of LinkedIn or a mobile device via the App.

- You will see the best matches for your search criteria initially, if you want to see more you can click on "See More" The filters will allow you to narrow down results and you can also use these to expand out networks later.

- When you find the person you want to connect with, go to their profile page and click on "Connect". You can, and should, personalise a note to them. Tell them how you know them, or why you want to connect.

- On a mobile device, once you are on the persons' page, click on the three little dots, then choose connect and personalise the note from there.

- If you want to remove a contact later you can by going to your Connections page, choosing Connections, then delete them by clicking on the dustbin icon. They won't be told, but if you want to reconnect with them in the future you will have to reinvite them to your network.

- Once connected you are "first degree" connections on LinkedIn (other connection levels are explained in more detail in Chapter 7 - Networking). You can now privately message each other, see each other's updates, posts and interactions and see who they are connected to, providing they are sharing their networks.

Now that you have a base network in place you can start to interact with them. Within LinkedIn you can make yourself more visible to your audience. Here are some simple ways to start, you will find more in Chapter 6 - Content Creation, and Chapter 7 - Networking..

- Use the "talks about feature", which you can add via creator mode. Add 5 hashtags that you are going to focus on the get active!

- Like posts and articles that your network share. The more active you are the more likely you are to move towards the top of search results. Activity involves joining and participating in groups as well as posting updates.

- You could write you own articles, use polls to gain interaction, share video clip or images.

- Find topics or articles to share with your network. You can share an update at any time from your home page and choose who to share these with.

- You can join groups and participate in discussion here too.

Company Pages on LinkedIn

A company page is different to your profile page as it promotes the organisation rather than you. You will be featured as an employee and a direct link to your profile will be automatically included.

Think about the company page as a free website! It will have its own URL which you can share to encourage people to follow it. You can publish from this page, send updates, add content, in the same way you can from your personal page, but your company page will not have its own network, but a number of followers. Anyone can follow you or your pages on LinkedIn so make sure your content is current, informative, and engaging. Also make sure it is kept up to date and share topical information that shows you keep abreast of your profession or industry with the latest news, reviews, and articles.

- Create your page, go to the "Work" tab at the top of the page and select "Create a Company Page" from the menu.

- Choose your company entity, size etc then follow the steps to start to tell the company story.

- Add in a logo, if you need to create one consider employing someone to help.

- Add in a webpage if you have one and make sure you fill in all the details required to make it easy for your customers to find you.

- Spend time on the "tagline". This is like your "headline" on the profile page. Make it simple to see what your business does.

- Tick the box to state that you are a verified representative of the company, and your page is now set up with these basic elements as covered.

- Now you can edit that page to really start to engage with your audience. You can access the page to make additions under the "ME" tab, you are the administrator of the page and can build the content, share posts, add custom buttons and invite people to follow. At the time of writing, you get 100 free credits to invite people to follow your page, so think about who you are targeting and aim for them!

- You can add Custom Buttons to drive business actions through your LinkedIn page. These may include actions such as "Register" "Contact Us" or "Learn More", but you will need to have a web page URL to drive people to. The button is just a link to push people towards your website where these actions can be taken. See Chapter 4- Website.

- Add hashtags!! Hashtags are like library systems to help others find your content. Think about the topics you want to be associated with or will talk about, add these # to your posts to increase the reach and engagement of your message

- Start posting content from this page. You can write your own articles on this page, share content from others and start meaningful discussions. Interaction is important on LinkedIn, not only from your company page but your page too. More ideas on what to share and how can be found in Chapter 6.

- You can get analytics on posts and visits to your page. You are going to invest time and energy into these sites, so you need to know what is working for you.

- You can give administration rights to another individual to help with the workload of managing your business page.

- Use the checklist included to make sure you have all the basics in place for LinkedIn to be a great tool for you to start to use in a professional capacity to grow your reputation and your business profile.

3   Getting Started with Facebook (Meta)

You may have noticed the name Meta popping up on some of your social media platforms. Namely Facebook and Instagram. Meta is the new parent company name for Facebook. Mark Zuckerberg wanted to rebrand the company and Meta was the chosen name as it "reflects the full breadth of what we do and the future we want to help build". It is also a reference to "Beyond" and the new Metaverse, where social media, augmented reality, and virtual reality meet.

At present there are no plans to rebrand Facebook or Instagram, but you will see the Meta logo starting to be more widely used.

Facebook is a great tool for reaching out to your audience of direct consumers. The site if often described as a business to consumer marketing tool. (B2C) rather than the business-to-business focus of LinkedIn (B2B).

Like LinkedIn you can have a personal page and a business or fan page and you can make another person administrator. Generally speaking, Facebook profiles are for people and pages are for organisations. They are treated as separate entities, so what you post on your personal page will not be seen by the followers of your company page. You can post and share personal things with friends and family, safe in the knowledge that potential clients or customers will not get to see this.

Like other sites you can use multiple media sources to get your message across to customers. You can write posts, add video, show work in progress, showcase your offices etc. by adding this content to posts and sharing with your followers.

Facebook covers a wide demographic of users, not just professional contacts and companies, but all ages, from teens to those in later life. So, if you have a certain target market there will be a strong likelihood that they are using Facebook.

Facebook is also a "sticky" site. Users tend to browse longer on this platform as it is a mixture of catching up socially, browsing adverts and often being drawn to pages because friends or family have "liked" them. Users tend to spend longer on posts as they feel more connected to the author.

In this section we will maximise what we can access and do for free to generate publicity and exposure. Facebook does have paid advertising services where you can target your audience by location, age, gender, interests and other factors. You can do this using the Custom Audiences feature to target existing customers directly or to increase your reach by using targeted advertising based on the algorithm of what your target audience browse, like and chat about.

You can access Facebook via multiple routes, via the internet on a tablet or PC, via the app on mobile devices. Each version will have slightly different features and accessibility to settings. Where possible use the full internet version to get set up, as it is much easier to set everything up with full visibility and the added controls detailed below. Here are some starting tips:

- When you think about using Facebook consider what your personal page says about you. If you are using your own name as part of your business or indeed feature as the Director/Owner or a key employee using your own name, curiosity may drive your customers to look you up.

- If you are happy to have your personal page out there for all to see, make sure there is brand consistency between the way you want to be seen and what your personal use of the site portrays, including images you use, what you comment on and what you share and post. Anything you do will form part of the impression your potential customers or clients develop of you and your services.

- If you are not currently a Facebook user, join via Facebook.com and create a personal profile page. Keep content to a minimum if you are not intending to use this tool personally. Then set up a business / fan page. See below.

- Use the name you wish to be found as and use your business email address. You will need to verify this before you can complete your profile and start using the site functionality.

- As with all sites, think about how you want to position yourself and keep the content professional.

- Fill in all the required sections, a full page will be more prominent in search results and also give a good account of who you are and what you do.

- Make sure you use a good photo, maybe the same one you use on other sites for continuity and instant brand recognition. Use an image in the background banner to add more interest to your page.

How do I connect with others?

- Facebook will encourage you to connect with all your friends, you can synchronise contacts with your address book but only do this if you really want to invite all those people to be your friends on the site.

- You can search for individuals by name, key words, job titles, etc the same way you can on LinkedIn. Just use the search bar on the home page.

- Once you find the person you want to connect with send them a friend request. They will hopefully accept, and you can then message them via Facebook Messenger, get visibility of their posts and shares and interact with them.

Who sees my information and activity?

- Check your privacy controls, Facebook allows you to quickly access your privacy controls across site to see who can view your posts, find you and interact with you at a personal level. To find this just go to your account settings, choose privacy makeover, and follow the steps on screen.

How do I set up a business or Fan Page?

From your personal profile you can set up a separate Facebook page, for free, to promote your organisation and invite your friends to "like" and "follow" your page becoming a "fan". See instructions below on how to set this up.

- You need to be logged into your personal profile page to create a Business Page. To create your page, choose "Page" from the menu and this will then instruct you.

- Add in background banners, a logo for your business or a photo of you to give the page an authentic feel.

- Consider the tagline, make sure you are consistent in the branding and message, refer to Chapter 1 for more ideas.

- Make sure you edit all the page info, filling in as many of the sections that you can as this will help to get you discovered.

- You can add in services, opening times, locations etc as standard in the page.

- Pages are split by classification and then by category; you choose which is most appropriate for your business to help you get listed in the relevant search results.

- You will be invited to tick the Facebook Pages Terms. Do read these prior to agreeing as you may decide not to continue or perhaps to be selective in the content you share.

- Once you have made your choice you will be guided how to populate and then publish your page.

- Make sure you check and critique prior to publishing.

- Company pages allow you to create various administrators to update your account without having access to your personal profile content.

- As administrator your name and personal profile will not show up anywhere on your page. Any content posted by you on your page will appear to be posted by your company not you personally.

- You can build content at your pace as your page will not be live until you publish it.

- You will be able to access your company page from the shortcuts section at the bottom of your home page.

- You can have an unlimited number of Facebook pages and an unlimited number of fans. (Facebook users who "Like" your page).

- Facebook Pages are public—anyone can find and view your page whether they are logged into Facebook or not.

There are lots of tools to help you to manage the content and interaction with your target market too.

- There is an area which is called the Business Suite as standard now on Facebook. From here you can access a whole range to tools including business apps, some are free to use, others paid, to help with online bookings and appointments or manage enquires via your Business Suite inbox.

- Add an automated message to the Business Suite inbox, stating how soon you will get back to your customers, this can help to manage expectations of your customers and clients.

- Your Business Suite inbox will allow you to see messages from Facebook, Instagram and Messenger all in one place as these are all owned by Facebook (Meta). It also allows you to see and respond to comments on both Instagram and Facebook.

- In Posts and Stories, you can schedule posts to release at a time you wish, and you can preload these. The added benefit of this is that you also get lots of free analytics to help you see what your audience like.

- You can use the online planner to schedule activity and also to draft posts that you may wish to edit further before sharing. Great if you want to review the administrators' contribution to the page before allowing it to go live.

- You can access paid advertising from this section, choosing the reach, demographic and finding something suitable for your budget.

- This area also shows insights to analytics with the reach, engagement and allows you to download reports.

- There are more tools to help with managing your page in "More Tools". In this area, you can see profanity filters to block any offensive language in posts, block certain words being used and show your posts in multiple languages if required!

Encouraging use or visits to your pages

- You need to become a "fan" of your page by clicking the "like" button and invite your friends and email contents to also "like" your page.

- Every time you post or a "fan" comments onto your page this post appears on the personal profile newsfeed of all your 'fans'.

- Use the discussion board and YouTube videos to add interesting content.

- You can use Facebook Ads to promote your business and they allow you to advertise a website. Go to Facebook advertising and click "create an ad" then follow the instructions. Or visit the Business Suite as mentioned above.

- Choose the landing page that your ad will point to, your ad's title, create ad copy, select an image then preview your ad. You can target you advert by country, demographics and people by likes/interests and connections on Facebook.

How can I use Facebook as a promotion tool?

- The real core of utilising Facebook to promote your business is to ensure audience engagement. You need to create and collate content that your audience wants to read and interact with. The algorithm on Facebook is tuned to this and will promote pages and users who create the most interest.

- Respond quickly to enquiries, comments, and shares from your customers and clients, show you are engaged with them and providing a real service.

- Word of mouth is still key to developing your business and social media allows you to speak to a wide audience. The more they like, share posts, or recommend you the better you appear as a provider of products or services, which increases trust, engagement, and promotion.

- All content posted on your Facebook page gets indexed on Google.

- You can target your posts by location and language.

- You can use the analytics as outlined above to see who is reading or interacting with your content.

- You can consider the paid advertising to reach your audience directly.

Facebook Pages or Facebook Groups?

In a few instances a Facebook Group may be a better option for you, or perhaps in addition to a Facebook Page.

- A Facebook Group is for a community of people with a common interest as opposed to a Facebook Page which is for a brand or entity.

- To set up a group, log into Facebook and click "create a new group".

- Fill in basic information and which friends you would like to invite plus complete your privacy settings.

Facebook Marketplace

Marketplace is an easy way to reach buyers. You can use the platform to sell anything from unwanted household items to new products or services, offer vehicles for sale and even houses to rent or buy!

It is simple to use, and you audience can find you using a range of filters including location, product and price.

- To set up a listing from your home page in Facebook, select the Menu icon ⠿ and select Create Marketplace Listing.

- Add up to 10 photos to make your listing stand out and take pictures at different angles, show the size where appropriate and use photos that really show your product off to its best.

- Fill in as much detail as possible in the sections of the listing. Make sure you choose the correct category for your products, there is a fairly comprehensive list that will help your buyers to find your products.

- You can hide the listing from friends if you choose to.

- There are certain products that are banned from listings you can see these on the Meta Terms and Policies page.

- To create a listing on the App, just look for the shop icon (Marketplace) click on the icon, choose sell and create your new listing.

- You can also sell in buy-and-sell groups. On the App you can discover nearby groups by using the filters, then join the group to sell your products.

- You can also do this on the internet version, go to the Menu, scroll down until you see Shopping and then you can access marketplace to see groups etc from there.

- Facebook does not have a payment mechanism within Marketplace. You will need to have a tool to facilitate payments outside of the platform.

As with any online selling platforms, you need to carefully consider how you will manage payments, delivery times, return policies, answer messages and so on. Find information on the technical and legal aspects in *100+ Top Tips for Setting up your Online Business*. See more at www.100toptipsbooks.com

You can also utilise Facebook to share video content through its "Watch" function.

Facebook Watch is mainly user generated content rather than channel broadcasting, like YouTube.

You could consider using this feature to communicate with your target market and here are some tips to do so:

- Anyone can add video to Facebook Watch, but you have to do this via your Facebook Page not your personal account.

- There is no guarantee your video will appear on Facebook Watch! You need to create several videos with meaningful content, that look and feel professional to gain interaction from your audience. This will work with the algorithm on Facebook Watch and increase your chances of being featured.

- You can increase your views by letting your followers know of new releases, therefore driving traffic to the clip.

- Perhaps create a series, to entice the audience to come back and view the next episode.

- You could promote the content on other platforms and share more widely, encouraging followers from LinkedIn, Twitter and so on.

- You will need to create you video outside of Facebook, you can use a mobile device or recording equipment, then edit using various software tools.

- If you use Zoom or Teams and want to record yourself talking about a topic or subject, you can record directly from these platforms and then download the video created to share or edit as above.

4   Twitter

There are several different sites which are classified as microblogs each has a limited space for your updates. Some are function specific for example financial, some are more hobby based. There are also sites in other countries which you would need to investigate if you are going to trade internationally.

Twitter is probably the best known in the UK, utilised by individuals, businesses, voluntary sector, celebrities, and communities. It gives you wonderful content for research and the opportunity to disseminate your content on an almost infinite basis.

You are able to post short messages (tweets) which are limited to 280 characters.

100 + Top Tips For Social Media Success

Twitter is a useful communication tool that allows you to interact with people around the world in three different ways:

- Send a short message to people publicly.
- Send a short message to a specific person publicly.
- Send a short message to a specific person privately.

Why would you use Twitter?

The organisation's use of Twitter is to meet potential customers and leads the same way you would at networking event or tradeshow. You can use it for the following:

- Develop and promote your brand.
- Interact with your customer base.
- Track what people are saying about your company and brand.
- Create a buzz around upcoming events.
- Help individual employees act as liaisons to the public.
- Promote other content you have created, including webinars, blog posts or podcasts.
- Develop direct relationships with bloggers and journalists for potential PR placement.
- Generate sales leads for your business.

How do you join?

Simply go to twitter.com and follow the joining instructions. You will be asked to create a Twitter "username" or "handle", so choose something that reflects your brand, not just a quirky nickname. If your name is your brand or company name, use this in the handle and use your name on your profile.

- Within the site you can add a short Bio or profile, just think about your strapline, make sure this is consistent with other sites.
- Add a photo and background banner, consider using the same images that you use on other social media sites or your website to maintain consistency.
- Add in location and a website if you have one.
- Twitter is also introducing "Twitter for Professionals" accounts with additional features. They will allow you to blog, post and interact at a professional level.

- Anyone who uses Twitter to communicate their brand, service or products can have a professional account.

- To do this you need to change your personal account to professional. Go to "Edit Your Profile", and switch to professional, you can then add the information you require.

- If you still want to use Twitter as an individual, you can set up a new account with the same email address, just use a different handle (username) and keep your personal use personal!

What do you write about?

Twitter is not about heavy-duty marketing as you will find that people will turn off very quickly. You need to work out your own strategy for what you are going to talk about, and when you are going to do it.

- Always add value with your comments – don't just tweet for the sake of it.

- Create a conversation strategy to give people a reason to follow you back and engage in conversation with you.

- Talk about things that interest them – not just to promote your business.

- Choose your topics carefully, you need to care about what you are saying. People can tell if you have a passion for your subject or are doing it for marketing.

- Always use hashtags in your tweets. This ensures a broader delivery of your content to a wider audience that my never have heard of you before.

- Be proactive, interact, to get more followers and recognition on Twitter.

- You can reply to tweets, using the icons under the original post. Use the speech bubble the circular arrows to re-tweet, the heart to like and the upload icon to share on other sites.

How do I connect to people on Twitter?

Twitter is a little different to the sites we have looked at so far in terms of connecting to others. On Twitter you can follow others and do not need their permission to do so generally. The etiquette on Twitter is that if you follow someone, if you are of interest to them, they will follow you back.

- To find people to follow, search on #topics, industry sector or any other key words you can think of. Look at the persons profile and decide if you want to follow them.

- You can also search by name as other sites and find people to follow.

- When you follow someone, you will get their tweets on your feed on the home page, and you can interact directly from there.

- So, make sure you choose like-minded people or individuals or companies in your target audience and share interesting and useful content to gain that interest.

- Don't expand too quickly – if you suddenly follow too many people at one time Twitter could pick you up as a spammer and may even suspend your account.

So how can I optimise my account?

- Consider how often you are going to tweet and plan it into your marketing schedule. Also consider who you will follow and how you can attract followers.

- Manage your tweets by using Tweetdeck.com or Hootsuite.com. These sites allow you to prepare content and plan the delivery of your tweets to suit your schedule.

- Use sites like bitly.com to reduce the length of URL links within your tweets.

- Use Twitter Lists to group your followers – check out how other people in your industry are grouping lists of followers. You can create two types of lists.

- Keep expanding your Twitter community – schedule time each week to maintain your followers and who you follow.

What else do you need to know?

Twitter content is very open and gives you great opportunities to research on companies, organisations at large, people and products.

- You can search on an organisation or individual by name and read their messages as well as see how many followers they have and how many they are following.

- Twitter also allows you to check what other people are saying about the organisation, product, or individual by inserting a hashtag # symbol in front of the word you are searching.

- You can search on any topic including yourself or your organisation name to see if anyone is talking about you.

- Twitter is great for complaints. Send out a message publicly stating your issue using a hashtag in front of the name of the company and product.

- The organisation will pick up the complaint very quickly as they search on their name for comments.

5   Pinterest

Pinterest is a visual social network where you "pin" your "interest" onto a virtual noticeboard. You create a "pinboard" which highlights some of your best visual content. This is not a site to sell products or services, but you can direct them to your website or other social media site. These pins could be:

- Pictures from a company event, infographics, data charts, eBook and book covers, photos of your products with your customers.

How to join

- Go to the website and follow the joining instructions.

- As with all sites make sure you are consistent with the image you use and the strapline you choose.

- You can add in a website or other social media platform.

- Similar to Twitter, you can convert your personal account to a professional account in the account settings, all followers, content shared etc will remain the same.

- You can have multiple accounts on Pinterest, and like Facebook, swich between these from your home page. Simply use the drop-down menu to choose the account you want to utilise and go from there.

How to start to use the site

- Start to create a few boards of your own to collect information.

- Create boards by clicking on the + button, you will see you can create a pin here, and at the top of this section a drop-down menu where you can allocate your pin to a board or add a new one. Always use clear, searchable names for your boards.

- Look at what others are using when you search for material, think how your target audience would search. What terms would they use? What # are popular?

- Follow the steps on the screen to create the individual pin, make sure you tell people what the pin is about and use #hashtags to get it found.

- Follow other like-minded users and pin some of their content to your boards.

- Add your pin button to your website and Facebook page.

- You can also download the pin button to your browser, so when you find content on any website you can click on the Pin icon from your toolbar and go straight to Pinterest to share.

- Many people use Pinterest on mobile devices, so the orientation of the image is important. Portrait seems to work best on mobile and try to avoid awkward cropping as this will lessen the professional look and feel.

- You can overlay text and add descriptive copy which reinforces the message. Good descriptions can help with SEO and encourage viewers to click through.

- Use different formats for your pins. Consider using video, single images or multiple images to keep the viewer's interest.

- Think about seasonality, topical subjects, trends and use these to your advantage when naming your boards and pins. Many big brands will use this tactic to make sure they are seen not just on their own pages.

Connecting to others on Pinterest

Like Twitter, Pinterest is more of an open networking site. You can find "pinners" of interest and follow them; they may well follow you back. Therefore, on this site we are building an audience of like-minded individuals not necessarily engaging with people we already know.

6   Instagram

When Instagram started out, it was simply a way to post pictures with your fans and did not have a lot of marketing value. In the last few years Instagram has proven to be an effective platform for marketers to reach a new audience.

- It's easy to share on Facebook, Twitter and other sites.

- Use your Instagram profile to make it easy for everyone to see your story.

- Instagram has over 130 million monthly users who generate over 1 billion "likes" so it is a real window to showcase pictures of your organisation or your offer and is a way to instantly capture the here and now and share the moment with others.

Joining the site

- You can join via the Instagram portal, just follow the joining instructions, and set up your account.

- Add a clear photo/image on your page and as always make sure your strapline supports your brand.

- Tell people what you do or offer by setting up a business account. If you do this you can add in an address field, use contact buttons, directions, email address and a contact number. Be accessible to your customers.

Managing your image

- You can either set your privacy settings to "Private" to show only your followers your information or set to "Public" to allow anyone to see your pictures and bio. This may help to reach new customers rather than just those who are already aware of you and your services.

- If you switch to a Business account, you will no longer be able to set your account to private. You'll also only be able to share your Instagram posts to the Facebook Page already associated with your Instagram account. However, you can switch back to a personal account at any time.

- Choose well composed clear images and be selective. Don't just add a picture because you can, really consider the overall impression and does this do justice to your brand/image.

- Consider the nature of your organisation for the style of shot you use. If your business is to sell a product, show it being used, if it's a service, show the service in action. Static images need to still showcase how or why you, or your product is the right choice for the customer.

- Think about what makes your business unique and try to capture that in your content, images, and posts that you share.

- Encourage interactions. Actively ask for people to take action, liking, sharing and commenting on your activity.

- Make sure you reply to comments on your posts in a positive timely manner.

Connecting to others on Instagram

Instagram will offer to synchronise your contacts. You can do this manually by tapping on your profile picture in the bottom right. Tap in the top right, then tap "Settings". Tap "Account", then tap "Contacts Syncing". Tap next to "Connect Contacts" to turn on contact syncing.

You can also search for contacts on the site by name, function, company so you can reach out to a much wider audience.

Like Twitter, you can follow people, unless their account is private, and receive updates from them. In terms of messaging directly people you follow you can do this by going to their profile page and choosing message.

Maximising visibility and impact

Look for peak times to add your images and monitor what is working for you.

- You can use Instagram Insights to see the best time to add photos for your audience. You will notice that your comments usually start to tail off about 8 -12 hours after posting so you need to make sure you hit your audience when they are most likely to be using/viewing the tool.

- You can add filters to improve the image and tags to make the photo appear in more searches. Using Instagram Insights will help you break down the best performance for your audience.

- Use only three to five tags per photo as you don't want to "spam" others who may not be interested in your offer.

- To see your Insights, just go to the mobile app, sign into your Business account, and select "Activity". From here you can see statistics on Activity, Content and Your Audience.

- Activity looks at profile visits, website clicks and directions. Content focuses on the performance of your posts. Audience shows the demographics of your followers (you do need more than 100 followers to get this) and also when they are most active on the site.

- The more you post the more interest you can generate. Follow other users, search for the tags you would want to be associated with or interested in and follow. People will then view you and follow you back if interested.

- Repost photos to other social media sites, you can link to Twitter, Facebook, and others as this will increase your following and exposure.

- Using these sharing platforms people may start to follow or share your images with their networks.

7   TikTok

TikTok is a short burst video sharing site. Typically, the videos are 15 – 30 seconds and the App has in-app editing features to allow you to create content on the go.

In the past it has been mainly used by individuals sharing their creative content with an age demographic of 16- 25. Now it is widely used by companies and small business operators to directly market their offer.

Consider your audience and competition, are they likely to be using TikTok? If so, you need to be on this site.

As of January 2022 TikTok has 1 billion monthly active users and 2 billion monthly active users worldwide, so the potential to get your brand out there could be huge.

TikTok is generally more relaxed than other more formal sites. Using emojis, avatars and sharing less than perfect studio produced content is OK on this platform, and in fact gives a bit more of that authenticity and personal connection. But, consider your brand and image and if this is right for you.

Joining the site

- Download the app to your phone. This is the best way to use TikTok as you can create video and share instantly via the mobile app.

Simply go to TikTok and follow the joining instructions.

- You can have a Business account and a Personal account.

- You need an email address to join or you can sign in via other social media channels such as Google or Facebook.

- You will be automatically assigned a username, but you can and should change this.

- Fill in the profile, include a photo, you can even include a video here, a short bio and link your YouTube or Instagram accounts if appropriate.

Using the site

- As TikTok functions are self-contained within the app, it is really simple to create and share your video content.

- Go to the + button at the base of your phone or device screen and click on this. You will need to give permission to the site to use your camera and microphone.

- Select the video length you prefer and record!

- You can add effects, features and even music to your video. TikTok has a built-in library you can use and you can save to your favourites for future use.

- You can save your post to draft or once you have finished upload straight away.

- Remember to help your video be found, use a description, add hashtags, @ friends, add links, you can decide who sees this and save to an album if you wish.

- When you are ready you can upload the video to the site.

- There are a number of paid advertising features on TikTok which could help your reach your audience, consider if these might work for you.

- Use #challenges! You can explain the challenge and promote your brand at the same time.

- You could consider approaching TikTok influencers to feature your products or brand, they may have millions of followers and have a great presence on the site, but you would need to come to some arrangement for payment. See chapter 4 for more information on affiliate marketing.

Does it work for you?

- TikTok has free analytics for Business accounts.

- Make sure you have set up a Business account to access this. If you have set yourself up with a Personal account, you can switch this to a Business one in your settings.

- You can view "Settings and Privacy" from the menu, then choosing "Creator Tools" from the account menu, then "Analytics".

- If you want to download the data you can do this on a desktop, sign into your account and from there hover over you photo and select view analytics.

- You can get an overview of how your account is performing for a certain date range. Choose overview from the four options to see this.

- Content, this can help you to see what is most popular with your audience again over a date range, and metrics for each post.

- Followers, will show you what is being watched and by who, in terms of gender and where they are viewing from.

- Finally, you can earn diamonds on this site! If you share live video, this can be monetised as you can exchange the diamonds for cash. You need to be over 18 and need a huge number of followers to send you these virtual gifts!

8   YouTube

YouTube is a free video sharing site where you can have both a business and a personal account. It is a great resource to showcase your business in action or products in an environment where they are designed to be used.

You can create your own channel where you can share your videos, invite others to subscribe to that channel and keep your audience updated or any new additions, product launches or promotions.

The site has around 2billion users worldwide, so it is a great way to reach a global audience with engaging video content.

YouTube is owned by Google so you will need a Google account to be able to set up a YouTube business channel. You can view content without joining the site, but not administer your channel.

How can I use it?

There are several different ways to use free space on YouTube.

- Set up your channel. Sign in using your Google account. If you don't have an account, you will need to create one.

- Once you have joined, from your initial at the top of the page, choose "Customise channel". Here you can add branding (photos and images) and basic information.

You have up to 1000 characters to use to describe your business and can add different languages.

- Add links to your site in the banner or in the main body of the channel to direct users to websites or other social media.

- Include contact details so potential customers can reach you easily.

Starting to share

You can use recordings from mobile devices or other promotional materials you have had made. You can even go live straight to camera if you are confident to do so.

Here are a few more ideas to help you get started. You could create videos covering:

- Demonstrating product features and how to use them.

- Tutorials, full and taster sessions.

- Building relationships, talking directly to your customers.

- Creative teaser campaigns.

- Offers and promotions.

- Recommendations, testimonials, and references.

- Case studies and examples.

- Before and after your service.

Remember you are projecting your brand to potentially millions of people so practice and critique to improve your performance before you go live.

How to upload content

- To upload a video you have created, click on the "Create" icon (video camera) you can then drag and drop the video. It will remain private until you publish it, then you can choose who sees it.

- Once the video is uploaded and saved as a draft you can edit the details. Add in a title and description, add in tags or sponsored links, a thumbnail image and most importantly select the audience suitability.

- There is an inbuilt music and sounds library which is free to use, and you can star your favourite ones to use at any time to enhance your clips.

- You can edit and trim your raw video in YouTube. Once it is uploaded in draft click on the thumbnail, then open "Editor", select trim and you can then remove the sections you want to omit.

- You can blur faces, add music, and even add an end page here to direct people to a website or add in a call to action.

- It is best to practice these techniques well in advance of sharing your first video. Remember you want the clip to reflect your professional brand.

Other areas to note

You may receive comments from your viewers as well as likes.

- You can manage comments from your side panel. It is a good idea to keep a close eye on this area and respond in a professional and timely manner.

- You can "grow with YouTube" and monetise your channel. You do need over 1000 subscribers and have had over 4000 hours of video viewed, the site will notify you once you meet the criteria.

- You can get analytics, go to analytics from the side menu and you can see your performance for channel and content.

- You can see data on views, watch time and subscribers from here.

9   Snapchat

Snapchat is a mobile app that allows users to publish photos that will automatically delete shortly after being viewed. Be aware that "delete" doesn't necessarily mean that it disappears before a screen shot is taken so be conscious that if you put something out onto the internet it is there, in essence, for ever.

People have shared more than a billion "snaps" since the app was introduced in September 2011, and currently more than 20 million snaps are shared every day.

How can I use it?

- You can promote your organisation, add coupons, and reach out to other users via this new short-term visual message format.

- You can share photos, video clips, locate people on snapchat maps, and even utilise/experience AR (Augmented reality).

- Businesses tend to use Snapchat to drive impulse purchases (60% of buyers tend to do this on the platform) so it's a great way of driving additional sales.

- Your snaps appear as a personal message rather than just an image, that has to be viewed, this may give a more customer centric, one-to-one feel to your audience.

- Consider your demographic with this App, most users are under 34 and it really is aimed at the business to consumer market. Check the current stats and audience before you start to avidly post.

- You can add stories to Snapchat. These last the site for 24 hours. These can be viewed repeatedly in that time.

How can I use it to capture customer details?

- Snapchat allows you to add friends via SMS so you may wish to canvass mobile numbers at the point of enquiry/sale. Do clearly state these may be used for marketing purposes and give customers the option to opt out.

- You can gauge how successful Snapchat campaigns can be by viewing your "score". This relates to the total number of Snaps you have sent and received.

- Under the feed page, tap the "Snapchat" header. Your score is the combination of the sum of what you have sent and viewed.

How do I get started?

- You need to start with a Personal account and then you can add a Business account.

- Snapchat is app driven, so use your mobile device to get set up. Download the App, then tap sign up and follow the instructions.

- Now you have a Personal account, go to the snapchat ads landing device and tap "Create account". As you already have an account, sign in using those credentials, then add in your business details and once complete you are set to go.

Navigating the site and its features.

- Navigation is through a variety of screens, you access many functions from the camera screen, which is essentially the home page. This is where you can take and send snaps, and navigate to the other areas of the sites using swipes.

- Swipe left for the 'Chat Screen". Start a conversation in this area, you can have one-person chats or you can use groups. In private conversations images and messages will delete when you end the chat, for groups they delete after 24 hours.

- Swipe right for the "Stories Screen". Here you can see your stories, friend stories and those from brands and creatives.

- Swipe up for the "Memories Screen". This is your library system for saved chats and stories.

- Swipe down for the ''Search" Screen. Here you can search the site for friends and content and check out what's trending.

- Look at what your competitors are sharing and the content they are creating then start your snapchat story.

- To create your snap, click on the round capture button at the bottom of the screen. You will see a red marker to show it is recording and you can record 10 second burst of snaps, if you keep holding it down you can create up to 60 seconds of content.

- Then you can get creative using the tool bar at the side. Add captions, doodles, add music, add weblinks to divert to other social media platforms or your website for those impulse buys!

- When you are happy with your snap you can then choose who to send it to, add to your story or snap map it, show where it has come from. This can be great if you are at a supplier, exhibition or somewhere else relevant to your business.

- You can add multiple snaps to create your story. From the snap click on "Story" then "Add".

- If you want to see your story later add this to your Memories. Do this on the camera screen, tap the profile icon in the top left corner, then tap the download button beside "My Story" to your current "Story to Memories" or your camera roll.

Analytics

Like all social media sites, we need to know our time is being well spent and to analyse this. At the time of writing full analytics is only available to influencers and brands with a large following that Snapchat has verified

To gauge how you are doing in the early stages you can:

- Tap on the "eye icon" in any story to see who had viewed this. Note that you can only see this when the story is still live.

- Use third party tools, some are paid, some will give certain analytics for free.

- These tools will help to measure stats such as completion (who has watched to the end), views, audience insights (demographics) and even compare to how you are performing on other social media sites.

10 The Future

Social media is ever evolving. It is key that you keep up to date with developing features and new technologies.

You may have noticed the development of VR (virtual reality) and AR (Augmented reality) with toys and gadgets recently. These are transferring into the world of social media and services. One example of this is being able to purchase high end fashion and wear it in a virtual world! You never own the item, but you can have as many photos in it as you want.

Tools such as Zoom are looking to tap into the virtual reality world adding advanced features which are compatible with Oculus VR headsets. Using these you can be "physically" present in a meeting, walk up to the white board and add your comments.

You can also use features on the site to place you and your clients in a meeting room environment. When you view the screen, you can be placed around a table, or in a lecture theatre depending on the numbers attending.

Snapchat has AR lenses on phones which overlay images and art onto pictures or can distort live images. You may never venture into this field, but this is just one way that social media is becoming even more interactive.

You may also have noted the rise in "Voice Notes" being used via WhatsApp and other platforms. These could be a great way to reach your registered customers via a dedicated voice note straight to their mobile device. If both parties are using the App the communication is free and direct.

QR codes, a quick response or two-dimensional bar code, are making a resurgence in the market. You can generate QR codes to signpost people to webpages and can create these in QR generators online. Use them on other media such as business cards, stationery, flyers, posters anywhere where you want your audience to be redirected to your online presence.

Social media is here to stay and will grow even further as more and more wearable technologies are introduced. This is fuelled by desire to keep updated, interact with others, review products, services and people or make purchases, wherever we happen to be.

Some useful sites to follow include: Social media examiner, Forbes, Wired, TED Talks

Search the internet for advances, regularly carry out searches for the platforms you are using to see what's new and help to keep your use up to date. If your audience can use the functionality you will need to too!

Use search sites like Google Alerts and set up dedicated searches on the social media platforms you use, enter an email address search for the site to send you updates as soon as information is released.

Chapter 4 - Setting up your Website

Having a website representing you or your organisation has many benefits.

- It means that your customers and clients can access details about your products and services at any time of the day or night.

- It is a cost-effective way of marketing and branding your organisation internationally with minimal extra requirements.

- You can update your customers about your products and services in one place.

- It can provide easy and effective customer support allowing them to communicate with you and vice versa.

- You can create income by selling direct to your customers, affiliate marketing, or linking to other e-tailers like eBay or Amazon.

To make the most of the opportunities available you need to understand the process of setting up a site and decide on the way forward. This could be that you start with your own DIY site, or you employ someone to build a site for you to update and then move on to employing someone or an agency to manage your site in the future. Whatever method is correct for you, it is worth knowing the basics before you spend time or money.

1 - Domain Names

The first domain name in history was Symbolics.com, which was registered on March 15, 1985. Today, there are more than 300 million domain names, with millions more added each year.

Your domain name is your website name, and it is what people will type into their browser to get to your website.

- Select a name that represents your organisation and is easy to remember, pronounce and spell. This could be your company name, your own name or even merging words that define products or services. For example: B&Q use the website DIY.com. Think about how you search for websites yourself.

- If you can incorporate a keyword, whilst still keeping your domain name short, this will be useful with regard to search engines. Avoid hyphens and double letters.

- Check if any other organisations are using your company name and if so, look at their websites to ensure that their professional image is not going to work against you. Choose an alternative name if this is the case.

- If you have a Limited company, use the Companies House website to check for companies with a similar name before registering your company.

- Once you have decided upon your company name you need to register that as a domain name so that it cannot be taken by other people. Be aware that even though you may think your domain name is original, it could already be registered by someone but not actually in use.

2   Domain name extensions

The extension is the combination of letters at the end of your domain name. In the past these were quite limited with country combinations, like, .co.uk or .eu and .com was the accepted international extension. This has changed and there is now a huge selection available.

- There are many domain extensions which reflect the content on that site such as .biz, .info, .co, (be aware that .co is also a country domain name for Columbia) through to .sport, .diamonds and .singles.

- If you are only selling products in the UK a .co.uk or .uk extension is useful to indicate to your customers that you are focused on the UK and products would be priced in pounds sterling. If you are aiming for an international presence .com or, the newer .global would be more appropriate.

- If you want to set up a personal site or a professional portfolio to showcase your skills and experience, then extensions like .me, .pro may work for you.

- Some extensions are country specific, such as .us, .uk, .de (Germany), .ke (Kenya) and you might need to satisfy certain conditions to register them. For some like .eu you need to live in the European Union to be able to register the domain.

3   Domain name registration

The "Registry" is the master database of all domain names registered in each Top Level Domain.

The non-profit Internet Corporation for Assigned Names and Numbers (ICANN) oversees the entire system of domain names, and it allows outside companies, called domain registrars, to sell and manage domain names.

ICANN has responsibility for Internet Protocol (IP) address space allocation, protocol identifier assignment, generic (gTLD) and country code (ccTLD) Top-Level Domain name system management, and root server system management functions.

Nominet UK are a United Kingdom based, non-profit organisation that manage the Registry of all .uk Domain Names, basically if you need a .uk ccTLD then this is the company that will be dealing with the registration of it.

- Some of the .uk domains managed by Nominet are: .uk, .co.uk, .org.uk, .net.uk, .ltd.uk, .plc.uk, .me.uk, .sch.uk

- As well as the .uk domain names they also act as the registration company for the following domain names: .cymra, .wales, .bbc, .bentley, .comcast, .telecity, .xfinity

Nominet now hold well over 20,000,000 .uk domain names making it the second largest registrar company in the world.

As well as the registration of domains, Nominet also deals with disputes about registrations of domain names which may involve mediating the relationships and issues between parties and the ownerships of the UK based domain names.

You will need to register your domain name through a registrar.

Registration agents

A registrar is the company or organisation that you choose to register your domain name through. This may be an Internet Service Provider (ISP), a domain name reseller or a company that specialises in registering domain names and protecting intellectual property and brand rights.

- Not all domain registrars have the license to sell all domain name extensions. For example, some domain registrars can only sell domain names with country-specific extensions.

- You pay for your domain on yearly contracts which can be for one, two, three or more years at a time.

- You can register your domain name with a registrar, selecting the extension/s you want if they are available and hold them until you want to prepare your website.

- Make sure you order your domain on an automatic renewal basis as, although the annual cost can be small, the loss of your domain name if you forget to renew can be high. The registration agent will contact you a month before your renewal date to remind you and you can cancel if you want.

- You also need to check for any additional fees for domain transfers, renewal, and other charges.

Some of the most popular domain registrars include GoDaddy, Bluehost, and Domain.com, although there are many more to choose from. Investigate pricing and policies for each one before choosing your domain registrar.

- Once registered you can move your domain name to another service provider if you want. This could be because they have a wider selection of offerings or because they are smaller and offer a more personal service.

- Companies like HubSpot, have software to design your website, manage SEO, and create a blog. Some options are free.

When you register a domain name with ICANN, you must provide your contact information including your name, phone number, physical address, and email address.

As soon as your domain name is registered, this contact information becomes available to the public — unless you pay for domain privacy through your domain registrar. This domain privacy will shield your information from view keeping your personal information safe from spammers or worse, identity thieves.

- Domain WHOIS Privacy allows domain ID protection.

4   Website pricing and Payment

The cost of a website can vary considerably. You can get free space from a number of hosts like WordPress and Wix but this can mean that you have their name in your domain name or their name offering a free service prominently displayed on your website.

If your site is a community service then this may not be an important factor but if you are trying to create and promote your own professional brand it looks "cheap" to say the least!

The standard costs of a website area as follows.

- Your domain name is paid in periods of one year after an initial fee. Dependent upon the extension, or promotion, it can be free up to in the region of £50 for a standard name being available. Premium domain names, .com or .global for example, are more expensive than other domain names because of what they bring to a website. This means a premium domain name has a higher page ranking in search engines and brings more organic traffic to your website. Reselling can add any amount to this figure, this is for the first year only. After this, the cost will be standard annual price as per the extension.

- The space that you need to host your website on is paid on a monthly basis and this can vary from just a few pounds to tens of pounds per month again dependent upon what you need. Don't be tempted to pay for vast amounts of space unless you need it. Standard information websites actually don't, for most websites with text and images, 3-5 GB should be sufficient.

- Choice varies from unlimited space with little or no human intervention – great for those who know what they are doing, to seemingly small amounts of space but with the option to be able to speak to a human for help.

- In addition, you have various options including shops, SEO, special business templates, mobile marketing and the ubiquitous anti-virus offerings. Only take what you need, you can always upgrade if you need additional services.

- There are no costs involved in setting up most social media sites links from your website.

- Should you want to place advertisements or upgrade then you will need to investigate the charges as well as researching the potential benefits prior to arranging.

If you plan to build the site using online web builders there are minimal costs other than time, however if you don't have the skills, you will also need to consider employing someone to build it for you. Costs can vary for example.

- Offshore company – £10 – £25 per hour.

- Freelance web designer – £25 – £50 per hour.

- Small web agency – £50 – £75 per hour.

- Large web agency – £75 – £150 per hour.

Depending on the type and size of website you need, you can expect to pay anywhere between £200 and £10,000 in total for a designer. Alternatively, the cost of building a website using a DIY platform typically ranges between £13 and £220 per month. There are some free DIY options out there, but they're only for creating very basic websites.

It's worth doing your research before making your decision on how, when, and where you are going to set up your website. A good site to get information with regard to all aspects is websitebuilderexpert.com. Taken from their site, they suggest.

- For the perfect balance of ease of use and powerful features, try Wix

- For the most professional template designs, try Squarespace

- For the quickest way to build a polished business site, try GoDaddy

5   Layout, presentation and branding

The presentation and content on your site encourages people to stay and to move around your pages which is a positive as far as search engine optimisation.

- The structure of your pages and overall site should be clear and easily understood. Use "breadcrumbs" on every page so that people know where they are.

- Select colours for your audience and offering. Don't go overboard on too many colours as your pages will become chaotic. Use two to four colours to start.

- Keep the style and layout of your pages consistent throughout your site. Your site needs to flow from page to page with navigation placed in the same location on each page.

- Keep animation and gadgets to a minimum. Only use to support good content.

Usability is important to ensure designs are effective, efficient and satisfying to use. Usability includes accessibility, which relates to ensuring equality of user experience for everyone. Many areas, like the EU, have penalties for failure to create accessible designs. There are additional benefits.

- Improved SEO (Search Engine Optimisation).

- Opportunities to reach more users on more devices, in more settings/environments.

- Enhanced public image for your brand.

- The World Wide Web Consortium (W3C) stipulates standards for accessible design in its latest Web Content Accessibility Guidelines (WCAG).

There are a number of easy methods to improve the user experience and accessibility. Here are some ideas.

- Use alt text on images.

- Describe links and add icons e.g.: PDF, or "click the square button".

- Use high contrast colours and select the colours carefully. Use tools such as WAVE and Color Oracle to test your design's accessibility.

- Use easily understandable content, focus on simplicity and clarity.

- Offer transcriptions for audio resources, captions/subtitles for video.

- Consider how screen readers handle forms.

A screen reader transmits whatever text is displayed on the computer screen into a form that a visually impaired user can process. Usually via a synthetic voice that reads text aloud, some communicate data via a refreshable braille display. A screen reader is frequently used by people with visual impairments or learning disabilities. It is also helpful for people learning English (or another language) and for the elderly. Screen readers help test accessibility because they confirm the flow of the page.

Fonts

There are many different fonts, and although there are some agreed areas regarding choice, others are still up for debate. The accessibility aspect is one to keep in mind, not just for the visually impaired but also those with dyslexia. Think about the following before choosing your font.

- Sans serif vs serif font. The difference between Arial and Times New Roman for example. Some sans serifs are actually harder to read than those with serifs.

- The weight of the font. Too fine may look elegant but it is harder to read. Italics are also difficult for many.

- The shape of the letters and the space between the letters "cl" can easily be misread as "d".

- When looking for the best fonts for reading, you also need to consider their availability for all users – Microsoft, Apple.

Check for details on fonts to use on the internet via the website for The Bureau of Internet Accessibility. Some pointers for you to consider:

- Aim for a font with a tall x-height, this is the height of the lower-case letters like m, a, x, and r.

- The height difference between lower case and capital letters, so that, for example, capital "i" and lower case "l" look different.

- Distinguishable characters, for example, L, l, and 1 should all look different from each other, as should o, e, c, a.

- Sufficient space between letters.

- Avoid thin weights on smaller font sizes, narrow width fonts, block capitals, italics.

- All headings need to be easy to differentiate, and different from the body text.

There are a number of well used fonts which are both easy to read and available.

- Times New Roman has become the default font for print and web documents. This serif font has a relatively small x-height, but it is excellent regarding legibility.

- Verdana is a sans-serif font that's widely used. It was created by Microsoft, is a popular font for accessibility and reads well on both web pages and digital documents.

- Arial is a sans-serif typeface. It was designed as a print font, but its open design also looks great in web design.

- Tahoma is another sans-serif typeface created for Microsoft. Similar to Verdana but with a narrower body, smaller counters, and tighter spacing between letters.

- Helvetica is a traditional print font available on Mac, Unix, and newer versions of Windows. The tall x-height makes this font easier to read at a distance.

- Calibri is a font designed for Microsoft. While it does have an x-height that's not particularly large, it offers a good distinction between most characters.

Different fonts communicate different messages to people. For example, a study showed that people are more likely to believe information written in Baskerville than Comic Sans.

Serif	Classic, traditional, trustworthy	Times New Roman EB Garamond
Sans serif	Modern, minimal, clean	Arial Lato
Slab serif	Bold, quirky, confident	Courier New Roboto Slab
Script	Elegant, unique	Dancing Script Petit Formal
Handwritten	Informal, artistic	Permanent Marker Patrick Hand
Decorative	Stylized, distinctive, dramatic	Fredericka Lobster Two

Fonts for online material should always stay at 10pt and above. Certain fonts also read easier, such as Arial, Georgia, Verdana, and Times New Roman.

One of the most important aspects in the design process is to ensure that any text you use is not only pleasing to the eye, but also easy to read. Like colour, fonts can be very expressive. Knowing your brand personality will make this process easier as well as getting to know the personality traits of each font category.

Simple. Clean. Powerful. Sans serif fonts are the most common and most versatile fonts out there. In the digital world, sans serif fonts are the font of choice for thousands of brands around the world, thanks to their clarity, legibility, and simplicity.

Colours

As already detailed in Chapter 1 – Creating your Brand. The colours you use to project your brand, write content on your website or even the backgrounds for your visuals are all important and can influence reactions from your audience.

Certain colours can trigger emotions and moods in people, others prompt urgency and some can instil calmness or nostalgia. Plus, there are many people who suffer from colour blindness so, this too, needs to be taken into account when you start using colours.

Colour blindness is also not just the simple red green which most of us know. There are three main types – Deuteranope, protanope, and tritanope. In comparison to regular vision, and in very simple terms, deuteranope and protanope struggle to see reds and greens in varying amounts, this includes oranges and purples. Someone who fits into tritanope vision has problems with yellows.

Search for how colours look to people with colour blindness so that you understand how your colour choices may impact on your customers. So, make sure there is a high contrast when using complimentary colours and consider the colour you use for your text.

However, bold black text on a bright white background makes it difficult to read if you are dyslexic causing a red haze around the letters. Many sites are now using dark grey instead of black.

There has been much research on colour psychology and how this can influence audiences. The interpretations of colours can be different around the world. Here are some simple explanations for the UK market.:

Red. The colour of power, urgency, aggression. It catches your attention quickly.

Blue. Trust, coolness, calm, reliable. The one colour which is visible to colour blind people.

Pink. It can be bright and sassy or soft and gentle. In the past it was typically female, not so today.

Yellow. Bright, confident, extrovert.

Green. Gentle, natural, environmental links and health. Also, a connection to money and wealth.

Purple. Known as the colour of royalty. It is rich, elegant and prestigious. Purple and white together is sometimes perceived as colours of mourning.

Gold. As expected, luxury, wealth and prestige.

Orange. Energetic, fun and attention seeking, a great accent colour.

Brown. Represents structure, security and protection. Serious and down-to-earth balanced with being reserved or even dull.

Black. Sophistication, seriousness, authority and sometimes depression and evil! Very useful but use in moderation.

Grey. Reliable, intelligent, classic but sometimes seen as boring.

White. Pure, innocent, clean, peaceful and a great backdrop to colours.

6 Building your site

You need to consider, plan and prepare your website to ensure it is right for your brand and will appeal to your target market.

- Think about what you are offering and who you are offering it to. Consider the price band, the expectations of your target market and what your competition is already doing.

- Decide whether you want to design it yourself or pay an expert to create your website, logo and images.

- Consider approaching tutors from the final year in design colleges to put your request up as a tutor led project with a prize. Plus, the student will then have the first professional commission of their career.

- If you prefer more expertise visit some of the sites where people tender their services to projects presented to them. There are a number of different sites, here are some to get you started. Upwork.com, Guru.com, Worksome.com, Fiverr.com, Truelancer.com.

- Information on how to create, manage and protect your website can be obtained from many commercial businesses online.

Website structure

Prepare a straw man prior to going live. List key areas of interest for your target audience and capture content to support topics. Once you have all the top-level content listed then dig deeper to find content to expand upon the topics. Only after you think you have exhausted all items that you would like to feature on your site should you start to build your content.

- Keep the style and layout of your pages consistent throughout your site. Your site needs to flow from page to page with navigation placed in the same location on each page.

- Make sure the structure of your pages and overall site are clear and easily understood. Use "breadcrumbs" on every page so that people know where they are.

- Keep your formatting simple. Use white space, bulleted lists, headers and short sentences and paragraphs.

- Select colours for your audience and offering. Don't go overboard on too many colours as your pages will become chaotic. Use two to four colours to start.

Uploading visual images

If you are including visuals, you need to save them at the correct size to ensure your website loads quickly. Research done by Google shows that, if a web page loads in more than 5 seconds, the probability that a mobile user will leave that page increases by 90%.

The speed that a website loads is also a ranking factor for SEO. The faster is your site, the better you can potentially rank.

There is image reducing software on Microsoft and Apple but you can find many sites which will compress your images for free like JPEG Optimizer, Kraken, TinyPNG, Imagecompressor, Ezgif.

You will be using images of different proportions and in different places on your site, these will need to be optimised appropriately.

Full Width Images that cover your whole screen from left to right, which could be hero images (oversized banner image at the top of a website), full screen slideshows or banner images. To ensure that your full width images look good across any device big or small the recommended size is 2400x1600px.

Inside Content Images, there will be sections consisting of images, text and call to action buttons and these could be portrait or landscape.

- Portrait - max width 1000px

- Landscape - max width 1500px

Slideshow Galleries - make sure your images are all the same height recommended 1500px, horizontal or vertical.

Blog Post Images – to upload images into a blogpost, they should all be the same width, recommended 1500px, horizontal or vertical.

Optimising and saving images for the web

Depending on the purpose, you need to save images in one of the following formats .jpg, .gif, or .png. JPG will be the most common format when saving images for your portfolio website, they will also be the lightest in size.

You'll want to label your images correctly for SEO purposes and you'll want to save them in the right colour format (sRGB for web).

Filenames need to be appropriate for each particular image or blog post. Use only letters, numbers, underscores and hyphens. Try to use only English letters. Characters from other languages, question marks, spaces, percent signs may upload incorrectly or cause unexpected behaviour online.

Image SEO

Once your images are sized, optimised and uploaded to your site you need to add ALT tags. The ALT tag is what search engines use to read images. Without them, your images are pretty much non-existent on the web.

7   Search Engines and key words

How do search engines work?

Search engines rank websites according to various criteria worked into complex algorithms. This includes content, keywords, links, ease of navigation, the number of views and how long they stay. Google is probably the biggest and most used globally so being aware of any changes that they specify is important to ensure you get to the best position possible.

To achieve the top position on page one is exceedingly hard and not guaranteed regardless of dedication. You may consider paying a specialist to optimise your site but being aware of the criteria helps.

- You need to ensure you deliver what the customer is looking for when they enter their words into the search engine.

- The people using search engines are the search engine's customers.

- If you deliver exactly what they are looking for and they stay on your site for some time the better the search engine considers your site, and you rise up the listings.

- Create your pages and write for your target market and not for the search engines.

- Write your content first and then check that you have sufficient keywords.

- Choose a primary keyword for each page and focus on that topic/word. Too many different keywords on a page confuses the search engines as there isn't a clear theme to the page.

- Be aware of your legal requirements – accessibility, data protection, terms and conditions.

- Be aware of the rules – duplicate content does not mean a higher rating on the search engine it can mean that you are pushed further down the rankings.

- Install yoast.com or the WordPress all-in-one SEO pack onto your website or blog. These will advise how to optimise your site legitimately.

- Set up a Google alert for "content marketing + SEO" and read anything it pulls back for you.

- Attend webinars that talk about content marketing and SEO.

There are numerous search engines available and they have similar ways of scanning the internet to return the site with the nearest results to what you have searched on.

- Search engines capture and save searches that have been made before and suggest ideas to assist you to find what you are looking for.

- To do this they are using your search data as well as others so anything you do on the internet can be captured, recorded and used by the search engines in the future.

- This content is also sold to various companies to market their products. It is used to send focussed marketing campaigns to the company's target market of customers.

- Consider the "incognito" tab on Google or use DuckDuckGo to search with added privacy. DuckDuckGo doesn't collect user data and track you when you search. Unlike Google, it doesn't associate what you look for online with your IP address.

- Using key words or phrases on separate pages to direct people to the right area of your site.

When you are planning your site, you need to think carefully about all the keywords which your customers will search for. The better the match the higher up the search results your site may appear. This is classified as search engine optimisation, SEO.

- There are codes and acronyms that companies use. An Airline may use a code for a certain airport, LHR for example, but the customer may search for Heathrow.

- Try to link key words or phrases to a particular section of your website, don't repeat every key word on all the pages, this will dilute your results or give a poor customer experience.

- Google search your key words and check the results, sometimes these can be different to what you would expect. If the sites returned are relevant, think about how to add these words into your own site.

- Remember search engines do not think for themselves! They simply match the words and content on your site and deliver the key matches back to your audience.

- One key piece of advice. Absolutely do not use white text to try to add in as many key words as possible. Search engines are now able to identify these and will block you from searches.

What is Boolean Search?

Boolean Search uses a combination of keywords and the three main Boolean operators (AND, OR and NOT) to organise and sift through your searches. It produces more accurate and relevant results, allowing you to navigate through appropriate candidates, while disregarding the unrelated.

The first important thing to appreciate about Boolean is that there are only five elements of syntax to understand. These are: AND, OR, NOT, () and ""

By applying these appropriately, along with the keywords you are interested in, you can create a huge range of search operations. There is no limit to how often you can use any of these elements in a search, so you can create very specific search strings, which will save you a lot of time in filtering the results.

Boolean methods can be used on any search engine: Google, LinkedIn, or even Facebook. Boolean is a term used to define the process of combining keywords with words called "operators." These operators tell the search engine how to use the keywords in the search.

AND / &

When to use – When you're searching for a someone and you want the results to include multiple keywords.

- Example – 'I want to find a freelancer who is a web designer
- Example search – Freelancer & Web Designer

OR / |

When to use – When you want the job description to include one of a number of keywords, but they don't all need to appear.

- Example – 'I want a freelancer or contractor'
- Example search – freelancer|contractor

You could follow this with an AND to include other words

- Example - Freelancer OR contractor AND website design

" " marks

When to use – When you want a job description to include an exact phrase.

- Example – "I'm looking for Website Designers".
- Example search – "Website Designer" (Searching website designer without quotations, for example, could bring back a number of other designers, such as interior designer or website developer).

*

When to use – When you want your search to start with a certain term.

- Example – "I want information on websites".
- Example search – web* (This will return all words which begin with "web", for example website, weblink, web design and so on)

( )

When to use – When you want to group two or more sets of conditions together.

- Example – "I am looking for website designer, specialising in online selling".

- Example search – "website designer" AND (online selling)

8 Earning from your site

There are different ways to earn from your website. They key ones are listed below.

- Selling direct, both products and services and you can link to other selling sites like Amazon and eBay.

- Affiliate marketing, where you earn commission by promoting another business's product or service. This could be for actual sales, leads or clicks on their website.

- Selling advertising space on your website.

Selling direct

Dependent upon what you are offering you need to decide whether to advertise what you will be charging. Some sites keep their pricing private and only share it with customers who ask, you need to balance this with how many people will not make the effort to enquire if they have no idea as to if your prices are high, medium or low.

Linking to other sales sites

There are many different sites which you can use: Amazon, eBay, Etsy, Facebook Marketplace and many more.

For most sellers, Amazon offers the most profit potential compared to eBay. Because Amazon is over 10X the size of eBay, the potential for sales is much higher.

Pros:

- Offers a huge customer base.

- Allows you list for free and is an excellent choice for major sellers.

Cons:

- Higher fees

- Fierce competition and competition with Amazon's own offerings.

eBay has grown considerably and is still one of the most popular sites for selling items. As an auction site, sellers are often able to get more than the item is actually worth. You also have more creative freedom when it comes to designing your product page.

Pros

- Size and reach with easy access for customers and you can target a specific customer demographic.

- Seller protections.

- Anything can be sold, and you can auction your products.

Cons

- Numerous seller fees. You pay for listing even if you don't sell your product, and again if you do.

- There is limited control over your listings.

- You will face significant competition.

Etsy is similar to eBay in the way they charge a listing fee. The positive for Etsy is that it allows listings to stay up for four months, eBay is usually 10 or up to 30 days for a fixed price.

Pros:

- A great platform for selling vintage and handmade products.

- Allows listings for up to four months, charges only a minimal listing fee per item.

Cons:

- Less traffic than eBay, and is niche-specific market.

Facebook Marketplace

Pros:

- Driven by the local community and doesn't charge any fee.

Cons:

- Doesn't offer the same protections as eBay, has the possibility of fraudulent offers.

Affiliate Marketing

This is when you promote another person's website and you earn from the promotion. There are three types of ways you can earn from this promotion.

- Pay Per Click (PPC) also known as Cost Per Click (CPC) this is similar to the way Google operates with AdWords. You get paid every time a link or an advertising banner is clicked on.

- Pay Per Sale also known as Pay Per Action or Pay Per Performance. You are paid commission or a set-up fee for the results for a sale or sign up. This payment is higher than for PPC.

- Pay Per Lead, also known as Pay Per Action or Pay Per Performance, is similar to Pay Per Sale but is earlier in the process. It is used when the sale requires a personal interaction with the customer e.g. mortgage advice.

Selecting the right scheme is down to personal choice.

- You should understand your relationship with the individual and if they can be trusted.

- If they are offering less commission but have a good reputation and you work well with them it could be better long term.

You can join a scheme through a network or directly with the merchant.

The Network:

- Manages the relationship with the merchants and endeavours to ensure you get paid.

- You should get timely updates on products or new merchants to give you the most profitable options. If you promote a number of sites from them there is just one log in area.

- However, you could be offered less commission than dealing direct and as they control the relationship with the merchant you could be their top performer and still only get paid standard rates.

Directly with a merchant:

- You choose the merchant and can give direct feedback.

- You could be offered more incentives or bonuses as you are working direct and can compare your performance against others.

- You could also earn more commission from them as they don't have to pay the network and you could get additional commission from signing up other affiliates.

- The downside is that if the merchant is a new or start-up company you may find that if times are tight for them you don't get paid.

In general:

- Any good scheme should have an affiliate log in area to track your performance. The number of clicks, sales, leads and the amount of commission. This will allow you to monitor your campaign results.

- There is also software available to allow you to generate specific links for each of your campaigns which will allow you to see which activity generates the most revenue.

- Check the Terms and Conditions. Some terms are restrictive and apply strict criteria on how your site looks and how their products are promoted. Consider how this could impact on your own organisation before agreeing.

For all types of earning from a website, it is essential to understand the regulation for any online business, which concerns the way in which online companies communicate with their customers. Under this legislation, if you're selling something online, you must:

- Display your business' name and address, contact details, company registration number and VAT number on your website.

- Make it easy for users to read your terms and conditions.

- Always be clear about prices, taxes and delivery fees, and the terms and conditions of special offers.

- Confirm every order by email – you can set up an automated email response to ensure this happens.

- Make it clear that all marketing emails and/or unsolicited emails that you send are just that.

- Make sure the sender of any communication sent by your company is identified.

- With any internet-based sites it is vital that you understand how to protect your privacy and who will have access to your information or data.

9   Pricing and accepting payment

When deciding on a price to charge you need to understand a number of factors to help your calculations. Check out your competition to give you an idea of accepted pricing, particularly when you are offering a service.

There are basically two types of pricing: Cost-plus pricing and value-based pricing.

Cost-plus pricing

Cost-plus pricing is perhaps the usual way to price a product. You need to understand the costs, breakeven and profit. You also need to consider what the item is worth to your customer and what your competition is charging.

Value-based pricing

Value-based pricing looks at how much customers value your product or service and are prepared to pay. For this method you definitely need to compare your offering to that of your competition. This comparison would include:

- Matching features.
- Levels of service or guarantees.
- The quality.
- Brand recognition and company reputation.

If you are selling services, you can also consider the buyers spending power and budget for your support.

Here are a few tips to consider when pricing services in particular:

- If you are offering consultancy or other services it is better to meet clients, identify needs followed by a written proposal rather than showing rates - hourly, daily or weekly on your site.
- Costs for other services like training sessions could be detailed as additional charges or costs because there are industry expectations on pricing.
- If your organisation is product based, then confirmed prices make it easier for your customer base.
- You need to understand your profit margin so that you can accommodate any special offers you may put in place.
- Special offers could include vouchers, discounts, 'bogofs' or taster sessions.

Additional cost factors

Apart from the very obvious costs there are also the hidden, slightly hidden or variable costs that could affect your final pricing. Consider the following:

- How will charging VAT have an impact on price?

- Can you keep margins modest on some products in order to achieve higher margin sales on others?
- You might need to calculate different prices for different territories, markets or sales you make online.
- Do you need to allow for possible late payment by customers?
- What are the charges for accepting payments – credit cards, bank charges?
- Consider your payment terms and keep an eye on your cash flow.

How do you accept payment?

Most of the information in this topic has been taken from websitebuilderexpert.com. Go to their site for more in-depth details.

There are a number of different ways to accept payment online. You could:

- Accept credit and debit cards.
- Add a payment gateway.
- Set up a Direct Debit/Standing Order.
- Use eChecks.
- Integrate mobile wallet payments.
- Send click-to-pay invoices.
- Install recurring billing software.

Credit cards

To accept credit cards you will need a merchant account which is a type of bank account which allows you to accept payments. They charge for their service and you can choose the cards to accept

When a customer clicks to pay for a product or service on your website the merchant account holds the funds while monetary checks are made.

- Customer clicks to buy.
- Merchant account checks whether funds are available.
- Transaction verified by card association: Mastercard, Visa etc.
- Money enters your business bank account.

- Usually, the money is held within the merchant account for a couple of working days while the payment is verified, authorised, and deemed secure.

Payment gateway

A payment gateway connects your website to a checkout system. It links your website to cards like Visa, Mastercard, and AmEx, either embedding a checkout to your website or redirecting your customers to the payment gateway's own website to complete the purchase.

Payment gateways, like PayPal, Shopify, and Stripe offer a variety of services tailored to different industries.

Direct Debit

With Direct Debit, your customer authorises you to collect money directly from their bank account whenever a payment is due. Direct Debits are good if you are collecting payments which vary in their frequency and amount.

Standing Orders

A standing order is an instruction your customer gives to their bank to pay you a fixed amount at regular intervals whether this is weekly, monthly, quarterly or yearly.

These can be useful if you are offering a service like gym membership or sending products on a regular basis. Your customer will need your bank account details and will set up a regular payment from their bank account into yours. Make sure you give them a transaction number or wording for you to be able to connect their payment to an individual.

Standing orders are easy to set up by your customer, they are also very easy to cancel.

eChecks

An eCheck is a type of electronic funds transfer (EFT) that relies on the Automated Clearing House (ACH) network to process payments. Funds are electronically withdrawn from the payer's account, sent via the ACH network to the payee's banking institution, and then electronically deposited into the payee's account.

With the electronic check payment method, funds can transfer domestically and internationally via local or global bank networks.

Mobile Wallets

A mobile wallet is a digital way to store credit, debit, ID, and gift cards so that purchases can be made using a mobile smart device rather than a physical card.

By 2023, it's predicted that over 1.31 billion people worldwide will have used mobile payment apps over the course of at least six months.

These apps store your bank card details on your smartphone, enabling you to make quick payments online. Apps such as Apple Pay, Samsung Pay, and Google Pay. There are other apps used internationally.

The majority of ecommerce platforms will provide your website with the ability to accept digital wallet payments within their most basic price plans.

Click to pay emails

You can invoice your customers via email, they can pay within a few clicks. It's one of the most time-efficient ways for your business to accept payments online. You can use automated invoicing software to send out numerous invoices quickly and without a fuss.

These types of software will integrate your website, the invoice payment form, and your customer database all in one place, letting you see who's paid and how much you've earned from invoices so far.

Recurring billing software

Recurring billing software – also called automated billing software – is ideal for subscription-based businesses because it allows your customers to pay automatically each time the payment is due

If you want to build an online store, then you should know that ecommerce website builders, such as Shopify, support the ability to send recurring orders, invoices, and subscriptions through third party apps.

10 Where can you get support?

Professional bodies

Professional bodies are now online so you can access their information quickly. The organisations that are available to provide you with advice vary across standard processes and also internet specific information. For example:

- Terms and conditions, data protection, disclaimers and legal requirements can be found at www.ico.com.

- Supporting information can be found at the Internet Service Providers Association website www.ispa.org.uk

- Accessibility guidelines – advice on how to ensure your site is visible to the colour blind and also those with sight issues can be found at; gov.uk/service-manual/user-centred-design/accessibility

- There are also sites to advise on marketing standards and guidelines including affiliate marketing plus how to create and protect your brand

Training sites

There are online training sites available which supply free training over a number of courses from traditional through to current technology

- Visit the Open University, BBC and search 'free training courses in xxxx' to give you up to date information.

- Many online training courses give you free content to upskill or refresh your knowledge. Should you want a certificate for future evidence you may have to pay for the exam. Have a look at Coursera, Skillshare, and LinkedIn learning.

Financial information

There are sites for venture capital, incubators to nurture your business and information, crowdfunding sites and details on how to set up a merchant account

News and Statistics

You can find numerous sites which give news on finance, industry specific content and information about the internet and how it works.

Marketing and advertising

There are a huge number of marketing and advertising sites.

Some give free advice; others will be looking at you as a potential customer so consider how much information you want to give them when they ask you to register.

- Institutes and sites which display information on various codes of conduct.

- Information on web design, practical advertising guidance, how to publish online surveys, viral marketing and blogs.

- Details about marketing plans and tools and how to promote affiliate marketing on your site.

Website

There are sites which take you through the whole process of creating a website including the following:

- Domain names, registrars and internet service providers
- Free website builders, training and website specification guide
- Logo and site design, keyword support tools and information on search engine optimisation including analytics and monitoring
- You can use YouTube to learn a multitude of skills including how to build a website or blog.

Social Media

As with websites there are online handbooks and guidelines which help you use the social media sites effectively.

- Statistics and analytics about all applications.
- Information on blogs – how to and site reviews
- Sharing sites in addition to the traditional

Various

In addition to the standard topics there are a variety of useful sites offering information and advice.

- How to mix new media with old – newsletters, fulfilment centres, business card content, secure online storage
- Information on how to create videos and podcasts, sites to download pictures, videos and music
- Some are copyright free and at no cost, others are priced separately

Job and job support sites

These sites offer more than the traditional job boards and agency sites.

- They may specialise in specific types of jobs – project management, jobs abroad, jobs for the over 50s

- Sometimes they focus on shared support with forums and shared space.

Chapter 5 - Blogs, Vlogs, Podcasts

1 Blogs and Blogging

Blogs (weblogs) started as online diaries and have been used for personal life content as well as detailing travels allowing the owner to share their experiences with anyone or for their own friends and family.

Research shows that the organisations benefiting most from business/organisation blogging are the ones that blog frequently and consistently. However, blogs can be time and idea consuming. Make sure you plan appropriately if you decide you are going to utilise blogs to support your organisation.

Remember that building a successful blog takes time, effort, and commitment. As with any presence on the internet you need to be sensitive to how your content could impact on the perception your customer base has of you, your business and your brand.

Before you launch decide on the following:

- Is a blog the right media for your customer base?

- Do you have the time and expertise to consistently post content?

    o Some opt for daily, which is challenging.

    o Average is weekly.

    o Fortnightly, monthly or cyclical are also options.

- Is there enough to write about? The length of a blog can vary but in general they are between 200 to 500 words.

- Where will you host your blog? Will it be on your website or another hosting platform? See this chapter, section 5 - Where do you host.

- Are you going to ask for feedback or communicate with your readers? This can be very time-consuming and has the potential to invite negative comments, but also gives you great information to build on.

- Do you want to earn directly from your blog, and if so, how?

2 Vlogs and Vlogging

Vlog stands for a video blog or video log and refers to a type of blog where most or all of the content is in a video format. Vlog posts consist of creating a video of yourself where you talk on a particular subject such as reporting or reviewing a product or an event. They are usually around five minutes in length but can be much shorter like on TikTok or much longer if appropriate for the content.

Vlogs can be straight at camera – cooking demos etc, or in different locations as in travel vlogs.

How do you become a Vlogger? Make sure you do your research and preparation before launching.

- Understand if there is a market for your content by searching YouTube and TikTok to see what's already there and how many views the top results have achieved.

- Watch and learn from your competition or other popular vloggers.

- Know how to present yourself to your audience in a way which is attractive to them and is comfortable for you.

- Investigate the equipment you may need, and the costs involved.
  o Camera with interchangeable lens
  o Tripod
  o Microphone
  o Lighting, essential for indoor recording and will enhance outdoor recordings
  o Editing software – or investigate the cost of professional editors

- Choose a style you are happy with and suit your market.

- Learn about how to edit your videos and keep your results consistent.

- Make sure you promote your vlog on your website or other communication methods.

- Keywords are as important in a vlog as a blog or website, learn about Search Engine Optimisation (SEO) to improve your vlogs' visibility when searched for.

- Measure your success and ask for feedback.

How to create your video

Most of us are fairly amateur with regard to creating full length videos however there is software available on virtually all equipment which can assist in clipping shorter sections of video together.

- If you can't do a full minute or two in one roll then use this equipment to fill the time with shorter sections while still promoting the story. Use Adobe or Wave.video.

- Keep videos short and concise – remember people have a very short attention span. Better to get them to view a couple of shorter videos than try one long one and not come back for more.

- To get extra advice and information either search via YouTube or go to the free training sites.

- Get a teleprompter app to help you "read" your content. TeleprompterProLite is easy to use app and downloaded for free on your iOS or Android device. There are other paid versions available.

Your video can be uploaded onto YouTube as opposed to hosting on your own site. This both saves you space but more importantly you will be found far more often as a response to searches on YouTube than you ever will via a search engine finding your content on your own website.

Video gives you a fantastic opportunity to engage with your customers and potential clients. Use images, videos and podcasts to add interest always themed to support your message. Keep them as close to your offering as possible. Good photos of real people out-values stock images.

- Use YouTube or TikTok to host your site as more people will go there to search for a video than will find your site via regular search engines.

- You can have your own channel using it to show off your products, who you are and what you're about, what you're up to and more.

3 Podcasts and Podcasting

Podcasts are rising in popularity and can also be used for a number of different options. You will find more information in the next topic.

- They are great for tutorials at low cost.

- As with videos you can give taster sessions, testimonials and demonstrate how you can support a company.

A podcast is a collection or series of digital audio files available for downloading or listening via the Internet. All podcasts are free to access, and most are available via many different apps. You can download recorded episodes or listen to live podcasts, through online software they are record.

Podcasting is a much less crowded and competitive space than blogging, as of January 2022, there are just over 2 million podcasts, but over 600 million blogs!

Being audio, it's both cheaper for equipment and probably less demanding to record on a regular basis than video. One essential is that whoever is going to record the podcast has a clear and natural speaking voice. Accents are great and add character, but the listener needs to be able to hear and understand all the words. Often, your unique style of talking and presenting will be a major draw for why listeners choose your podcast.

One thing to take into account before you start is, as with Blogs and Vlogs, you need to be dedicated to creating a regular flow of content to build up an audience and then to retain your listeners. Your listeners will expect new material scheduled regularly.

Before you commit you need to plan.

Choose your topic, make sure you know enough about the topic and have a genuine enthusiasm for it.

Decide on the name which needs to be memorable and portray what your podcast is about. Have a look at the top podcasts charts to give you ideas and avoid duplication.

What will be the format of your podcast? You could always use the same format or mix it up on different occasions. Think about the organisation and planning involved.

- A single presenter or multiple hosts.
- Interviewing a guest who has a shared interest or knowledge.
- Storytelling.
- A combination of the above.

Cover art creation. Your cover art is the first impression most people will see as they browse through their chosen podcast app, so it needs to tell a story about your content.

Intro and outro music and content. Introducing the episode – name, theme, hosts. Outro to close with a thanks, usually a call-to-action (CTA).

Equipment selection

- A good quality microphone. It doesn't need to be the most expensive, you can always upgrade if your podcast is successful and you know you are going to continue.

- Investigate a podcast starter kit, especially if you plan on having a co-host or two. They can be for smartphones, USB with microphone or a combination. Have a look at thepodcasthost.com for more information, advice and training courses.

Audio recording & editing. There are many options for audio recording and editing software. Some high-quality software is free.

- Audacity and Garageband are free.

- Adobe Audition and Logic Pro are popular paid recording software.

Investigate how they work before committing, as if you haven't used editing software before, even simple actions can be quite intimidating and full of jargon.

Alitu is a "podcast making" tool that automates a lot of the technical elements, and almost builds your episode for you. It's all based inside your browser, so no software to download, and it works on any computer connected to the internet.

4   Where do you host

You can host your content on your own website or various accepted platforms. Unless your website has a huge following it would be better to host on a standard platform and link back to your own website so that you benefit from the audience volume already using the major platforms.

Blog Hosting

You could place your blog onto any blog hosting site, WordPress and Blogger are the biggest worldwide. Similar to using YouTube for videos more people will go to these sites to find a blog to read than necessarily will land on your website. However, there are considerations to take into account.

Hosting your blog on a free platform's URL like WordPress or Blogger means that the SEO benefits get applied to the blogging platform, not your website.

You can integrate your organisation blog with your organisation's main website. In this case the ideal home for your blog is on a sub-domain of your main website (e.g. blog.yourwebsitename.com).

Or put your blog in a folder of your main website (e.g. yourwebsitename.com/blog). Both of these options will allow your corporate website to benefit from the SEO your blog will generate.

Vlog Hosting

Vloggers are people who have a video channel on which they periodically upload content. A YouTuber records videos only for YouTube, while Vloggers use different platforms, the key ones are listed below.

YouTube. YouTube is big! It has to be the number one platform to consider. YouTube has over 2 billion users worldwide and over 500 hours of videos are uploaded every minute. YouTube being the most popular is highly competitive. Don't be put off, be creative and consistent and you can gain an audience.

You can create your own channel on YouTube, uploading content is straightforward. YouTube allows you to monetise your channel by putting ads in your videos.

Instagram. With a userbase of over a billion users, Instagram increased in popularity as a photo-sharing social media platform. Now, with the introduction of Instagram Reels and Instagram Video, vloggers are there too.

Vlogging by using Instagram stories is relatively new and is a good idea. To vlog on Instagram stories simply film your content and begin to upload it as multiple stories. You can add music, captions, and fun GIFs over your stories.

Short videos are trending nowadays, you can use Instagram Reels to upload shorter clips of your vlog to grab your audience's attention. Adding to that, Instagram Live and Stories will allow you to create a stronger bond with your followers. With Instagram Video you can share longer vlogs.

Facebook. Facebook is often overlooked for vlogging. However, its popularity and extensive user-base can prove highly useful for getting more exposure.

With Facebook, you can create pages, gain followers, and run paid ad campaigns to increase your visibility. It allows you to live-stream your videos with Facebook Live, save live videos to the video library, and interact with your audience in real-time.

When you create a vlog and upload it to Facebook, it assures a guaranteed reach within your friends' or followers' list. And if they share it with their own friends, the reach of your vlog multiplies instantly.

TikTok. TikTok has proven to be the fastest-growing social media app with over 1 billion users.

With short videos ranging from 15 seconds to 10 minutes long it's an ideal platform to host your shorter vlogs, as the popularity of short videos has increased. There are filters, you can add soundtracks, and various special effects.

Vimeo. If you're a professional vlogger or aspiring to become one, Vimeo is the place to showcase your creativity. On Vimeo, you won't see any low-quality content as it's known for its high-quality artistic videos. The platform even has tutorials that can help you make better videos.

As a vlogger or a content creator, you can track how your content performs using the analytics dashboard. You can get this feature and as well as more storage and advanced privacy control by upgrading to one of the premium subscription plans.

On top of that, there are no ads. And if your content is really good, your vlogs can get featured in a Staff Pick.

Podcast Hosting

Most podcast hosting is absolutely free. Make sure you check before you start. Hosting is available for Android and Apple, the listener can access across platforms.

A podcast host is where you store and distribute podcast audio files. They also provide analytics, web players, scheduling tools, and other features to make publishing and growing your podcast easy.

There are many different hosts, some are listed below. Buzzsprout is one of the easiest for a beginner but search which suits you.

- Podbean, Captivate, Transistor, Castos.

Once you have found a host and uploaded your podcast, they provide a podcast RSS feed to Apple Podcasts and other podcast directories.

A podcast directory is a listening app where listeners find podcasts. Podcast listeners search for, subscribe to, and listen to your podcast using their podcast directory of choice. Popular podcast directories include Apple Podcasts, Spotify, Amazon's Audible and Google Podcasts.

5   How long and how often?

There is no frequency which is perfect for blogs, vlogs or podcasts. It really does depend upon your audience and content.

Check your competition. How often and how much do they share, balance that with how much time it's going to take you and what you expect in return. This could be increased sales, awareness of your brand or just sharing good information. Think hard before you commit as all options can be a challenge.

Before you launch any of the options, prepare more than one event so that you have time in reserve to prepare future sessions. Prepare multiple offerings and keep them to fill the times when your time is short, or inspiration is lacking.

Blogs

There are many suggestions about frequency varying from 1-2 times per week up to 4-5 times per week. Several studies suggest that between 11-16 per month with 11 being the ideal.

Although your blog length may vary depending on your topic and audience, it is often best to aim for about 1,500 to 2,000 words for articles or posts.

Vlogs

Daily vlogs are the most popular today which, because they are short may still be manageable.

They usually last around 5 minutes, but some are much longer. Most times the shortness gives value without being too demanding for the vlogger or the viewer.

Podcasts

Most podcasts are released on a weekly basis, but it's also possible to have daily, monthly, or other frequencies.

The length of a podcast often depends on what you have to say and who you're saying it to. Often commuters listen to podcasts while travelling, so it's suggested to aim for 20 to 45 minutes. However, if someone is interested in your topic the length is not that important. Balance the time you spend to what you gain.

6 Feedback and communications

Feedback can often be a highly charged area and it's tempting to try and avoid giving people the option to comment. Ignoring the trolls out there, you can build huge audience loyalty. If people are engaged, they tend to stick with you and give you valuable information for free and there are other benefits to two-way communications.

- Comments on your blogs impact strongly on SEO, networking and traffic benefits.

- You can survey your readers, watchers and listeners from time to time to ensure you're still making content they connect with.

- Promote your content in online communities where your target audience visit. They could be communities on Facebook groups, Slack, Reddit, forums, etc.

- Ask questions on your social media platforms, post messages in a forum.

Get Transcriptions of podcasts, search engines will then "read" your podcast episodes and add benefit to your SEO.

To improve your quality and the potential to get more contacts you could also join a course relevant to blogging, vlogging or podcasting.

What about the trolls? It's hard to read negative comments and even harder if you have a dedicated individual trolling you or your business. The most important, as with most confrontation, is to think hard before you react and there are different approaches you could take.

- Ignore Them.
- Acknowledge the commenter's misunderstanding.
- Engage in thoughtful debate.
- Admit when you're wrong and apologise.

Similar to ignoring them, don't feed them either. If they're trying to be funny, your response could be just what they want for their pending punchline. If you don't respond, there's no joke. If you do respond, keep your cool.

7 Earning from your content

Earning can either be an instant financial return or increased following leading to a longer-term increase in your business. There are a number of different ways to get a financial reward, for example:

- Sell products directly.

- Affiliate marketing

- Advertorials and sponsored content.

- Charge for social media posts.

- Write for other sites.

How do you optimise your blogs?

Affiliate Income is one of the easiest and most common ways to make money from blogging. You simply promote other people's products on your blog, and when someone makes a purchase or sometimes just click on the advert they have on your blog, you make a commission off it.

- To get the best return from creating a blog you need to ensure your content is timely and topical.

- Review your business and marketing plans to understand any cyclical impact on your organisation and assign each subtopic idea to a date.

- Use content and supporting keywords appropriate for your target market.

- Add an RSS (Really Simple Syndication) button so that your blog can be subscribed to easily by readers.

- Also add an option to subscribe via email (don't forget your email marketing legal requirements – unsubscribe link etc.).

- Give every blog you publish a social sharing button so readers can share your content. Standard buttons would include Facebook, Twitter and LinkedIn plus other social networks according to those your audience use.

- Tweet links and post content to Twitter, Facebook, LinkedIn, and other social media sites your audience use.

- Pay regular attention to your blog analytics, regular visitors, subscribers, comments, page views, inbound links, tweets/retweets, conversions and any other key measurables specific to your business.

Making money as a vlogger

As with blogging, there are different ways to earn from a vlog.

- Advertising, when every time someone sees the ad or clicks on it, the vlogger gets paid. This means the larger your audience the more you can potentially earn.

- Depending on your vlog topic, you could charge viewers a subscription fee. This is not for all content types but cooking vlogs and specialist expert advice could work.

- Affiliate marketing is the most common type of collaboration between vloggers and brands. Promoting products or brands and offering discount coupons to your audience. When they are redeemed against a purchase you would get an agreed percentage of the cost.

- Sponsored content is the most lucrative but hardest to get. You will need to have a substantial following before approaching larger brands.

Can a podcast make money?

Podcasting is not a quick way to earn. You need to build a loyal, engaged following willing to buy what you're selling and even then, it could still be slow.

Sponsorships are the most common way podcasters make money. This is when the podcast promotes the sponsor during the show. You can also earn through affiliate marketing, donations and selling your own merchandise.

- Sponsorship. When your podcast becomes successful it will draw the attention of advertisers that will pay you to plug their products in ads that air during your show. Sponsors target shows with at least 5,000 downloads per month (only 10% achieve this). If your podcast is niche and aligns to the advertiser's target market, you may still attract a sponsor.

- Affiliate marketing is when you refer your listeners to specific products or companies. Transparency regarding the fact you would earn from your audience's purchase is essential.

- Donations. It sounds strange but you can ask your listeners for donations, particularly if your business is connected to a good cause. Equally, in return for specialist offers like exclusive episodes or live chats.

- Merchandise. This could be your own products or it could be promoting your brand/concept through branded merchandise promoting your logo. If this is the case you will need an e-commerce store and a method to manage stock. Sites like Shopify can host your store, help you with products and manage the logistics around fulfilment and stock control.

8 Security, protecting personal information

There are risks attached to blogging, vlogging and podcasting for your business. Your company's reputation, infringements of intellectual property rights, liability for defamation or illegal content and sharing confidential information in error.

Your site could be vulnerable to hackers and plagiarists. They may install malware to redirect your audience to their own sites.

Also, do backup all your content, just in case the worst happens and you lose whatever you have out there. If your content is safely backed-up, you can always republish.

Blogs

Popular hosting platforms attract hackers, be prepared.

- Secure your login. Change any default username.

- Don't share information about the version or theme you are using.

- Always back up your content just in case you get caught.

- Use as much password authentication as is offered. It takes more time but worth it to protect your content.

- Research how to guard against copy/paste.

- Set up Google Authorship to protect content you have published and has been copied and published by another site.

- Only install trusted plugins. Check the number, rating and reviews users have given the plugin.

- Install security plugins and limit login attempts. Plus, a firewall which will scan your blog for malicious codes.

Vlogs

With any type of video content, you may be inadvertently showing private information in the background. Think about details. Will viewers be able to see written correspondence, work out where you live, see photos of friends and family who don't want to be viewed, the list goes on and the impacts could be devastating if you get it wrong. You need to be aware of the potential for negative or harassing comments from so-called trolls, it can be unpleasant.

There is also the element of your account being hacked, Google has recognised that thousands of YouTube creators have been compromised over the past couple of years. Two factor authentication can help keep your account safe.

For example, cryptocurrency scams and account takeovers.

- An email is sent to your YouTube that appears to be from a real service—like antivirus brand with an offer to collaborate. They can impersonate established companies and large organisations.

- They propose a standard promotional arrangement, promote our product and we'll pay you a fee.

- If you click the link to download the product this will take you to a malware landing site and you will download the malicious software which will then allow a hacker to access your site and upload information.

- Google is aware of this and will require YouTube creators who earn from their channels to turn on two factor authentication for the Google account associated with their YouTube Studio or YouTube Studio Content Manager. Also take heed of Google's safe browsing warnings.

Podcasts

The possible security issues with podcasting almost mirror those for blogging and vlogging with (at the moment) no other specific areas to target within a podcast. So, it's basically about following all the safety advice and being aware of the dangers.

9 Copyright and legalities

There are a number of areas where you will need to investigate to ensure to do things correctly. The phrase "ignorance is no defence" echoes strongly across the internet. If you break the law you are still liable even if you have no knowledge of the law being broken. Do research and get legal advice when you don't understand.

Refer back to Chapter 1, Topic 5 – Protecting my Brand, for information on Intellectual Property which talks about, Trademarks, Patents, Copyright and Trade Secrets.

Consumer protection

The Consumer Protection from Unfair Trading Regulations 2008 prohibits certain practices. For example, using editorial to promote a brand when in fact it's content which has been paid for.

There are a number of authorities which oversee advertising and they strive to ensure that all advertising should be legal, decent, honest and truthful, be prepared with a sense of responsibility to consumers and society and not mislead, cause harm or serious or widespread offence.

There are limits in the actions they can take in terms of financial penalties, but it's damaging to your reputation if you are investigated by these organisations.

Collaborations between vloggers and brands can give rise to problems if the brand has paid and the vlogger does not make this clear in their video.

The following steps should be taken to ensure advertorials do not fall foul of the rules:

- Your viewer should know they are looking at an advert prior to opening a video which has been supplied by one of your collaborators – you could have advertorial or ad feature in the video title.

- Do not use grey phrases like "in collaboration with", "with thanks to" and "supported by".

When you have followers to your blog, vlog, podcast or website you will be in control of their contact data which means you need to be registered with the Information Commissioners Office as a data controller. See ico.org.uk.

You need to ensure you have their consent before processing their personal data in any way.

Copyright

Copyright is one of the main types of intellectual property. It allows the copyright owner to protect against others copying or reproducing their work. Intellectual property gives a person ownership over the things they create, the same way as something physical can be owned.

You can add a copyright disclaimer to your content, an example would be: Copyright @ [name & year]. Any illegal reproduction of this content will result in immediate legal action. Like in the example, your YouTube copyright disclaimer can just be the copyright symbol (or "C" or "Copyright"), it is recommended to add an advisement against theft to further protect your intellectual property.

100 + Top Tips For Social Media Success

The following information is from the UK Government site www.gov.uk/copyright it is worth looking at all the information they have published and keep up to date with any changes.

"Copyright protects your work and stops others from using it without your permission".

You get copyright protection automatically - you don't have to apply or pay a fee. There isn't a register of copyright works in the UK.

You automatically get copyright protection when you create:

- Original literary, dramatic, musical and artistic work, including illustration and photography.
- Original non-literary written work, such as software, web content and databases.
- Sound and music recordings.
- Film and television recordings
- Broadcasts.
- The layout of published editions of written, dramatic and musical works.

You can mark your work with the copyright symbol (©), your name and the year of creation. Whether you mark the work or not doesn't affect the level of protection you have.

Copyright prevents people from:

- Copying your work.
- Distributing copies of it, whether free of charge or for sale.
- Renting or lending copies of your work.
- Performing, showing or playing your work in public.
- Making an adaptation of your work.
- Putting it on the internet.

Copyright overseas

Your work could be protected by copyright in other countries through international agreements, for example the Berne Convention.

In most countries copyright lasts a minimum of life plus 50 years for most types of written, dramatic and artistic works, and at least 25 years for photographs. It can be different for other types of work.

Contact the IPO Information Centre if you have a question about international copyright.

10 Suppliers

Managing your online presence is a huge undertaking, you have to consider designing, developing, and managing your entire online presence including your website and social media platforms. All are vital components and require unique skills.

Time spent on your internet presence is time taken away from your business. Plus, do you have the expertise to cover marketing, advertising, content and engagement? If you are unsure then you should consider hiring experts. Before you jump in think about the following:

What do you want them to produce?

- Social media presence like Facebook, LinkedIn etc.
- Website creation, content, maintenance.
- Marketing email newsletters.
- Blogs, vlogs, podcast creation and production.

What is your budget.

It may be that it is beneficial to employ an agency or individual to get you started and that you can keep going once created. As with any work, you will need to research set up costs and ongoing costs and how financially beneficial it will be for you.

How will you measure success?

Increased business, increased engagement (likes on Facebook etc).

Klout is probably the best-known social scoring tool. It gives a score from zero to 100. A score of 100 is nearly impossible to achieve.

Kred scores people on a scale from zero to 1,000.

- Above 500 is above average
- Above 600 is in the top 21.5%
- Above 700 is in the top 5%
- Above 750 is in the top 1%
- Above 800 is in the top 0.1%

Where will you find them?

For individuals, LinkedIn, Glassdoor and other job boards. But also look through Hootsuite's Certified Social Media Consultants Directory. Do an online search to find out if there are experts out there who specialise in your area of business.

There are also a number of sites where you can find freelancers with a variety of expertise. Upwork.com, Guru.com, Worksome.com, Fiverr.com, truelancer.com

How do you know they are any good?

Ask them for examples of past work. Check how their accounts look and their follower numbers.

Check their social media accounts – look at how many people follow them. Do people interact with them?

Check which major social media tools they use - Buffer, Hootsuite, Oktopost, or SproutSocial.

Try and find out if their "likes" are purchased. Social Media Examiner wrote about how to spot a spammy Facebook page.

Chapter 6 - Content creation and use

1 Generic content and style

Great content, whether for websites, social media blogs, vlogs or podcasts is very similar. It needs to have the right combination of quality copywriting, user experience and overall trustworthiness to convert visitors into leads and keep your audience interested. Key areas to address:

- The quality is good. No spelling, grammar, pronunciation or knowledge errors.

  - The content is meaningful, insightful and unbiased.

  - Whatever you are talking about needs to be easy to understand, without being dumbed down or patronising.

  - Unique in the way it's written or presented.

  - Subjects gain traction if they are interesting and inclusive in their style.

  - Topics which help people do/understand/learn something.

Be observant, capture ideas, quotes, anecdotes and information you come across during your life to use in your blogs, vlogs and podcasts.

2 Visual imagery

Most picture posting sites will allow you to add imagery of your choice with comments making your products or services viewable by a huge audience. In todays' instant society we crave information that we can access and absorb quickly.

- The aim of adding visual content is to instantly build rapport with your audience. Choose images that tell a story.

- Try to think about the reaction of your audience before you add images. Will it help them to see what your product does, realise the benefits, or help then to engage with you? If not, don't post it.

- Get your users to be recognised! Add their user submitted photos – free advertising of your product – and they will start to view your posts more frequently to see if you have used their photos.

- Use the # to link your images to other areas of interest. If your product involves flowers, pet care, training solutions, use these as "# subject " so that anyone who searches for this will see your images. Make sure that they are relevant for all audiences and don't mix the # as this may devalue the content.

- Use images to put a face to your organisation. This helps to build rapport and allows your customers to see who they are dealing with (consider adding a team photo).

- If you don't have your own content and not keen to go down that route you can either get copyright free or paid content via a number of different channels. You download the clips you are interested in and clip them together. Until you have paid you will see a copyright watermark running through the clips. Once paid for they are all clear.

- Dependent upon where your images are going to be used, website vs social media platforms, you may need to compress your image sizes. For more information see Chapter 4, section 6 – Building your site.

You may decide to use these images to create dialogue with your target audience. You could run a "choose your favourite" or "what do you use yours for" type captions to encourage audience participation. This can be really useful if your product comes in many colours, flavours or is multi-purpose.

3   Written content

Content needs to be interesting, informative and add value for your target market. This is relevant wherever your content is utilised for example your website, blog or any social media updates.

When you have created and understood your brand and offering you should always keep a consistent approach to the content you give wherever that content is based.

- Speak directly to your audience. Use 'you' and 'your' as well as 'I' and 'we'. Write to help them solve their problems.

- Avoid corporate speak and jargon.

- Give and share information. Add information which educates and informs will support your professional position.

- If you ask questions, be prepared to respond quickly.

- Check your spelling and grammar. Be consistent, don't use a mix of English and American spelling.

4   Audio

Podcasting is a unique tool which allows you to deliver relevant, on-demand and targeted content of your choice to a worldwide audience. See more content in Chapter 5 – Topic 3.

- Research free online training courses to learn how to create podcasts. Or search on YouTube for advice.

5   Video

The content needs to be focussed on your target audience and the presentation needs to take this into account too.

Think about what you want to say and check out the competition before you get started.

Videos and podcasts can be used to promote a multiplicity of goods and services it can:

- Demonstrate a product. What it looks like, how it works, the size, colour, texture. How to fix it, pack it, and even how much it weighs.

- Customers will see how fabric moves, the finish on clothes, what it looks like on a real body with a real person telling the story.

- Clients can relate to how a consultant promotes their skills and expertise. They can assess whether they can work with the person (or not!).

- Customers can leave testimonials and recommendations which are more likely to be believed than just a selection of text.

- You can give taster sessions with regard to your services.

Video results

A Forrester Research report has indicated that video is 50 times more likely to appear on page 1 of Google search results than your website.

- Not many organisations use optimised video content, so competition isn't high.

- People are drawn to video and therefore Google keeps serving it up.

- Google owns YouTube. It's no coincidence that your YouTube videos will appear high on a Google search.

- Video SEO has many benefits over normal search engine optimisation.

- Videos are displayed above normal organic search results.

- Videos have to be self-submitted to Google meaning less competition.

- Better messages can be given in a video.

- Google and many other search engines are evolving and going past the basic web page search to include images, video and other media.

6   Website content

Your presentation not only needs to comply with all the accessibility regulations it also needs to be clear and easy to read for everyone. In addition, the presentation should support your brand and be consistent with all your visual content.

- Keep your formatting simple. Use white space, bulleted lists, headers and short sentences and paragraphs.

- Fonts should be easy to read both in terms of size and colour.

- Use images, videos and podcasts to add interest always themed to support your message. Keep them as close to your offering as possible. Good photos of real people out-values stock images.

- When people find your website it will probably be via a search engine. To ensure your website rises up the search engine rankings you need to ensure your content corresponds to the words your potential customer is searching for.

Unless your site is purely an online sales site there is a multitude of content which you can present to the world.

- Ask yourself: Will people arriving on my site know instantly what I am offering?

- Use clearly defined tabs to allow quick navigation and help your audience find what they are looking for.

- Do they know where they are on my site and how to navigate to other content?

- Is the content on the landing page relevant to the words searched for?

- Know your subject. Don't include anything which you are not sure is accurate. Include evidence – facts, numbers, percentages etc.

- Within your content offer access to eBooks, podcasts, whitepapers and videos.

- Add a sharing widget to every page so that people can promote your site for you on the various social media platforms

- Keep animation and gadgets to a minimum. Only use to support good content.

7   Social media content

Start by creating a profile or bio to show who you are, what you do, what services you offer, remember to be consistent.

See Chapter 1 -Building Your Brand and Chapter 3, Top Tips for Using Social Media.

Most of us are familiar with liking, sharing, and commenting on content created by others. Often content is "doing the rounds" and you soon switch off when the same repetitive posts and articles appear across your chosen platforms. Here are some tips to keep it fresh:

- Use news amalgamation sites e.g., Google Alerts to scan the internet for content on any topic you choose. Simply go to the site enter your key words.

- You can set filters to regions (these are global), sources of information, i.e., news, video, blogs etc, and choose the time scale. Daily for up to the moment, weekly for the best articles from the internet.

- Choose what you are going to share and set up a file for these links. You may not want to share everything at once. When you do, tell the reader why, what is good about it, why is this noteworthy?

- Your content you share should be Meaningful, Informative, Necessary, and Directed at your target market. Remember the acronym "MIND" before you hit send!

- Twitter lets you to share across other sites, you can link a LinkedIn account to a Twitter feed to share simultaneously.

- Use "mentions", quote the originators in your posts, tweets, and shares, this shows you appreciate their content and if it is "MIND"ful so will your audience.

- If using content from the internet in this way, you often see share buttons on the sites. Use these to allow you to add commentary around the article and share directly across your chosen platform.

- Don't forget to utilise video! You may not want to make your own, but you might find some good content to share on YouTube or other sites and want to pass this on to your networks. Remember, add in the WHY you are sharing this.

Many people want to create their own content rather than piggyback on others. All sites will allow you to do this.

- Generally, what you post, share or like, will be seen on your connections, followers or friends' feeds. To reach a wider audience use #Hashtags.

- Hashtags are library systems that make content easy to find by anyone interested in that topic. Try adding 3 different but related hashtags to your content to reach an audience that may never have heard of you before.

- Include links to your website or other social media platforms in your posts to drive traffic to other sites, and maybe capture details, enquiries and even sales.

- You can always use the sites to post directly your own written content to your network, followers, groups or other users usually directly from the home page.

- In LinkedIn this is known as "start a post", on Twitter "what's happening" and on Facebook "what's on your mind". Whatever it's called this is your way of creating short messages (content) and sending it straight away.

- You can add polls, to get interaction, video clip, images, weblinks in fact anything you want to include you can do from this area on you home page on the chosen site.

- You can create your own questions for polls, good for engaging an audience, you can choose how long the poll is active for and use this to reach out to all participants. Great for quickly canvassing views and opinions that may allow you to strike up further discussions and possibly meetings.

  o To set up a poll look for the little Bar Graph symbol. Usually, you will find this when you draft and update or post.

- o On LinkedIn you will find this when you use "create a post", the symbol appears on the bottom line.

- o On Twitter, you will find the symbol under "what's happening" where you would create your tweet.

- o On other platforms this function is usually part of your communication or story. On Instagram, look in "Your Story". If unsure use the help section of your chosen platform.

- o When you create your poll, you can ask a question with chosen responses for opinion or feedback. Your network would be able to see scores on the voting, but no who has voted for which option.

- o You can set the duration of your poll to make sure your target market has a chance to respond.

- If you want to write longer blogs, updates or newsletters or author your own posts, LinkedIn has an inbuilt area to do this and will help you to make it look professional.

- On LinkedIn go to "start a post" and just underneath this you will see "write an article". Click on this and you will be presented with a template article to fill in. You can add hyperlinks, images, video clip and really bring to life the subject matter.

- Consider how long writing your own article may take. Also, if you write something engaging and gain lots of followers, it is because they are expecting more!

- Break down large topics into chunks. Release one a week, or one a month depending on how frequently you are going to write.

- You can use scheduling tools such as Hootsuite to plan when you want to post or share content, Twitter allows you to-do this within the site as do some of the others. This will take the pressure off remembering to share or tweet as this will be fully automated.

- Be human! Don't be afraid to tell stories on these platforms, people engage with other people so you could share career stories, why you do what you do, what makes you proud and so on.

- Share hints and tips, give your audience something useful, stand out as a professional in your field!

- On image sharing sites such as Instagram, you might want to share before and after photos. Especially if you are in a creative field such as hair and beauty, dog grooming, upholstery, or restoration.

- You could also capture the progress of a project or activity in stages and share the challenges and problems you have faced along the way and then show the finished article.

- Consider promotions and giveaways if appropriate for your business. Facebook is a good platform for this as lots of people will share offers with their friends again increasing your reach.

- You could live-stream. Facebook Live is a ready-made platform to do this. Just ensure you advertise when you will be live, what you will be talking about or sharing so people know when to join.

- Post a variety of content that is related to your business or organisation. If you are a coach, share wellbeing stories, success stories, share inspirational quotes.

- Try to end your posts with a question, a call to action. If you have shared top tips for something, ask the audience what their top tip would be.

- You could select monthly topics, related to the seasons, i.e., Christmas, Diwali, Autumn, Winter etc and use images to engage with the reader that reflect the time of year or special events.

- See what others are doing! Look for examples of best practice. Search the sites, which pages inspire you and why, what do you or would you interact with and what makes drawn to those pages?

How will I know if this is working?

- All the sites will have free analysis tools you can use. Make a note of which posts, or content gets the most attention, shares or re-posts and make sure you include more of this in the future.

- If you use scheduling tools you can usually connect to 3 social media accounts for free, any more than that you would need to subscribe. These scheduling tools will also have inbuilt analytics for you to view.

8 Blog content

Blogging is hard work. You need to publish consistently, promote your articles, network, and more. If the words are flowing, write several blog posts at one time.

Remember, to write well requires practice. The more you write the easier it becomes. This does not mean that the quality is guaranteed so do get feedback from someone you trust.

- Write about topics people are searching for by using a free keyword search tool e.g., Keyword Surfer, Keyworddit, AnsweThePublic, Keyword Sheeter. There are many to choose from.

- Make a list of categories that could be of interest to your audience then make a list of 5 to 10 subtopics that relate to each category.

- Make your headline infinitely readable. Most people are attracted by interesting headlines, but make sure your content matches to expectation.

- Write so that people want to quote or reference you.

- Content should be unambiguous and easy to read. Short sentences and avoid waffle.

- Write guest posts for other blogs and ask other bloggers to write for you.

- Interview industry experts or a member of the public who has first-hand customer experience in your field.

- Don't be afraid to admit that you have changed your opinion about a subject from the past. It's a way of demonstrating that you are open to new ideas.

- Add photos and images to your blog content to increase engagement and interest in your posts. These could be:
  - Charts or graphs
  - Cartoons
  - Infographics
  - Curated lists
  - Industry-related book reviews
  - Q&As

The best blog topics for making money

- Finance
- Fashion
- Travel
- Marketing
- Health and Fitness
- Parenting
- Food
- Lifestyle

9 Vlog content

A vlog is designed to share experiences, thoughts, and ideas with an audience. It is a form of visual communication which is used to engage an audience interested in a particular topic.

A good first vlog post is one where you introduce yourself, the topic you will be vlogging about, and explain why you want to vlog about it. Share this information confidently and in your own style, this is when your audience will make their mind about if they will stay watching.

The first 15 seconds need to capture interest, attention spans are getting shorter all the time. Many vlogs are around 20 – 30 minutes with 15 minutes being the minimum for success with the YouTube algorithm. This is a long time to fill, without gaps and in a professional manner, on a regular basis, particularly if you have committed to a daily deadline.

People will be watching and listening to "you" so you need to be yourself and use words and a style which you would normally use.

Talk to the camera like you are talking to a friend, looking into the lens.

Be aware of mannerisms which could be off-putting or irritating, how often have onscreen journalists waved their arms so much that you have stopped hearing what they are saying.

10 Podcast content

Podcasts are listened to from the beginning, as opposed to someone dipping in part way as they might for a radio programme. This allows you to tell more complex stories and focus in on a particular topic.

You need to be able to talk about your subject for multiple episodes and your topic needs to be broad enough to entertain a wide variety of people. Start focussed and you can expand your topic later as your popularity increases.

Create a template that you can reuse every time you record a podcast episode. This would include your intro and outro music, a space for ad spots and tracks for your voice recording.

- Think about who you are talking to and give them what they want and expect. Speak directly to listeners. Be spontaneous, conversational and less scripted.

- Don't assume people know your presenter or programme, add introductions to welcome new listeners.

- Create a sense of community by cross promoting other podcasts, let them know so that they can reciprocate.

- Thank people for listening and also for any feedback you have received. Ask for reviews and recommendations in your outro.

- Tell your listeners about what to expect in the future and refer back to past episodes, if relevant, so that they can catch up if they missed it first time round.

Blog, Vlog and Podcast Ideas

The selection of topics is enormous, some ideas are listed below and they could prompt further subjects to choose.

- Travel: travelling, information about countries, customs, moving home, regulations.

- Technology: how to, reviews, experiences, history, future options.

- Tutorials: education, full and taster sessions covering academic, leisure or business.

- Motivation: challenges, inspiration, expertise, mindfulness.

- Music: knowledge or expertise, classical through to current.

- Demonstrations: products, skills.

- Health and wellbeing: exercise, food, diet.

- Beauty: makeup, fashion, hair.
- Relationships: business confidence, family, children.
- Case studies and examples.
- Recommendations, testimonials and references.
- Building relationships, talking directly to your customers.
- Creative teaser campaigns.
- Offers and promotions.
- Before and after your service.
- Interviews: experts, users, business owners.

Chapter 7 - Other networking tools

1   How to network

Use messages to Networking is important as our existing networks can help generate leads via recommendations. There are a finite number of contacts we can utilise; therefore, we also need to reach out to and engage with those who may never have heard of us before. Avoid the cold calling where possible.

Social media is the pathway to opening opportunities to social networking. Simply having a presence on these sites is not going to generate new interest in you or your offer. Networking will allow you to find contacts, connect with them and interact in this virtual world. You should still aim to gain physical discussions and short networking meetings where possible, as you can do so much more in a 20 min chat than you may achieve in a brief email exchange.

These meetings whilst "in person" can still happen virtually. With the introduction of Zoom and the wider use of products such as Teams during the Covid19 pandemic, virtual attendance at meetings can feel like being present in the room. Using cameras, screen sharing, whiteboards, and discussion rooms you can replicate those live meetings.

Networking is not about hard selling, using 60% of your interactions to share, inform, guide and advise and just 40% of posts advertising and selling your services is about the right balance.

Here are 4 key things to help you to effectively network and maximise your time:

- Select a few key associations or organisations and participate actively.

- Arrive early and stay late. You won't be able to network while meetings are in place, so look at the list of attendees in advance and see who you want to meet or interact with.

- Identify and chat to those you have met before. Remind them where you met and what has happened since.

- Share leads and contact where appropriate and non-competitive. Be generous with your thoughts, advice, and information. Give something to others and they will usually gladly reciprocate.

Bear these tips in mind as we start to explore how to reach others via the social media tools available.

How can I start to reach out to my Network?

It is important people know how to find you and can contact you quickly. There are some quick wins that you can deploy to allow this on most sites. Here are a few examples:

Add your social media buttons

- You can add active links to all your social media using quick links.

- Download the buttons from the sites you use and add these to email signatures, web pages, social media accounts, drive traffic to your pages.

- You can copy the code and embed these into your pages, and this will look and feel professional as the logo appears as a link to click on.

    Use A URL in your signature.

If LinkedIn is your preferred platform, you can:

- Add an automatic signature to the end of your organisation emails to direct people to your LinkedIn account. You should find this in your settings of your email account, and you can put in a badge from LinkedIn to allow people who receive your emails to click through and view you. You can find the badges in LinkedIn in the "View your Public Profile" area.

Here is how to do this:

- Go to your settings, select manage my public profile then click on "the create a profile badge" link. Simply follow the steps on the site to copy the code into your email automatic signature. Note: this only works for emails using outlook or on your blog or website.

Check the current email systems that support this function, it will only work on "professional" email systems such as Outlook, not Gmail, or other free accounts. If you are using an unsupported mail provider you could just add the URL to your email signature, see below.

Edit and Communicate Your URL

All social media sites will provide you with a unique URL or 'uniform resource locator'. This is your webpage and is unique to you and most importantly this web page is available on internet searches. So even those who are not users of the platform themselves can view your pages via the internet search engines. Most sites generate this at random, usually using part of your name and a few numbers. Try these tips to get your URL working smartly for you:

- You can usually find this function in your settings, or the profile/bio page. If not use the help section on the platform to direct you. Search edit URL and you should find simple step by step instructions on how to do this.

- To edit your URL on most sites, click on edit profile, then the word 'edit' next to your existing URL (usually under your photo) and change it to something shorter and more business-like. Then save your new URL to use.

- You can add your 'URL' to your business cards or promotional materials to direct people to your profile.

2   How Do I Find Networking Opportunities

Networking is about two-way discussions. When you are trying to broaden your network, you need to identify a "hook" to appeal to your chosen network contact. Look at discussion boards, news articles, and industry information to try to find a common topic or theme that you can get a network connection talking about.

On any platform you can search by name, job title, company, sector, and so on. The important thing to do here is when you find these new contacts, you personalise the invitations to them.

Say who you are, what you want, why you might be of help to them or what they might be interested in. Remember, personalising notes is not a long message, some sites restrict to 300 characters, so you need to prepare these messages wisely.

Within LinkedIn you can search across your network for free up until a 3rd degree level of connection. You may see on LinkedIn when you search someone has the number 1,2 or 3 next to their name in the search result. This denotes how far away they are from you.

If you see some with a 1st degree next to their name these are people you have connected to on LinkedIn by either accepting and invitation from them, or they have accepted one from you. You can message them privately, view and use their contact details, you will receive updates on their activity, posts etc in your home feed. You can also see who they know (if they have not adjusted their privacy). The people they know are your 2nd degree connections.

If you see someone with a 2nd degree next to their name, they are a contact of your 1st degree. You can view their profiles, send a connection request, but that is about it until you connect. The people these 2nd degree connections are connected to are not visible to you directly as these could run into millions, but you might see people with a 3rd next their name in the search results. These are a contact, of a contact, who is connected to someone in your contacts!

Here is a simplified example of the degrees of separation. Degrees of separation on LinkedIn are a bit like a pyramid.

Your First-Degree connections = 10

10 contacts (each has 10 connections of their own)

10X 10 =100, Your Second-Degree Connections = 100

100 Contacts (each has 10 connections of their own)

100 x 10, Your Third-Degree connections = 1000

100 2nd degree contacts (each has 10 connections of their own)

Using this scale, you can see the power of networking. The more first-degree connections you have the more visibility of others you have across the platform. If you want to see beyond the third degree you can, but you must become a premium member to do this. Look at the site for the latest fees and features for a premium subscriber. You may be able to do a free trial to see if this is of use to you before committing a monthly fee.

Search for Connections

We covered connecting with people in chapter 3, so recap this chapter if you are unsure. Once you have a base network in place you can:

- Use a variety of searches to find the right people to reach out to on LinkedIn. There are some useful free advanced tools or filters as they are known, you will see these at the top of your page once you search.

- In "All Filters" you can search for people with a certain job title, in a certain location, by industry, so this could be a very powerful way to find the right contacts and have an "IN" to begin networking with them.

- You can also use these filters to see who has moved from one company to another, using past and present company as your filter choices. This could be useful to see who has moved to target companies from organisations or contacts you had strong links with.

Groups

Groups on LinkedIn only share content, posts, and interactions with other group members. There are no longer public groups on the site.

- Every group in run by an individual or team of administrators. You will need to request to join the group. The administrator will then approve your membership and you are good to go.

- Using LinkedIn groups will help you to identify potential network opportunities.

- Use the search bar at the top to find suitable groups, put in the industry, sector, function or titles of the people you want to network with and select Groups from the filters.

- You should select groups that potentially have members who are your target audience. Once you join a group you can see who the members are.

- When selecting the groups look for those that are active and have a healthy membership level. If you are joining a group to see who a good contact for you may be, try looking for people who are actively discussing topics.

- If the group is to promote yourself or your offer, choose an active group to make sure you are going to be seen and your discussions contributed to.

- The members tab will show you who is in the group, and you can do a general search on key words to try to identify new contacts.

- Use the discussion threads as an "in" to start a conversation with someone. If you add to the discussion this can be seen online by all group members.

- If you want to reply to someone in private or contact them directly within the group, look for them in the group members list. As long as they have not changed their privacy, you should be able to click 'send message' to talk to them in private.

- You can use "Polls" in the groups, and this is a good way to start to engage with an audience and when people contribute to your Poll, you could follow up with a direct message.

- You can direct message any other group member, but be subtle with the direct marketing and sales pitch, you don't want to alienate yourself from the group.

Events

LinkedIn allows members to create online events. You could attend other people or organisations events or plan and run your own.

- Use the search bar to find events based on your industry, sector, etc. Register your attendance. You can then see more about the event and who is planning to attend.

- Create a list of interesting people, then use the attendance of the session to introduce yourself and make that contact.

3   Networking on Facebook and other sites

All social media sites allow interaction between members and provide great networking opportunities. These interactions are often seen on our landing pages as a "feed" or "thread".

Simple actions to take:

- Make sure you are optimising your profile pages. Remember when you interact, people will want to see who you are and what you do.

- Choose if you want to interact as an individual or from your business or fan pages.

- Make sure you are in the right account and posting to the right audience!

Now you are ready to start to network

Hashtags #

Hashtags are a feature on all social media sites and can really help you to get your content seen and help you to find people who already have a common interest. So, hashtags can offer you a ready-made, highly engaged audience.

Essentially hashtags are library systems, grouping together content.

Here are some ways to use hashtags on sites:

- First of all search on the #topic in the search bar at the top of the page.

- Find from the dropdown menu the hashtags in use and view them. See which has the most followers, use these to gain the broadest coverage of potential viewers.

- Add the relevant hashtags to your posts, you can add multiple hashtags to boost who sees the post.

- Follow the hashtags yourself to see what others post and share and of course to interact with them.

- Use hashtags in articles you might personally author. Look for others who have written content about your chosen subjects. You could reach out to them and start a conversation based on that post.

Get Started with Interactions

- Look for interesting content on your feed from people you want to network with.

- Interact - like, comment or share / retweet or Quote Tweet their posts. This gives both of you more traction with the sites search algorithm and increases visibility for both parties.

- Reach out to the author and thank them for their post or share. Tell them what you found useful or informative and see if you can secure a discussion with them. You will need to be friends on some sites, on Twitter you can generally reply to any user directly and in private.

- Post questions, you can then pickup with the individuals that comment and strike up discussions.

- Use Polls on sites for great ways to quickly canvass views and opinions that may well allow you to strike up further discussions and maybe lead to meetings.

- To set up a poll look for the little Bar Graph symbol. Usually, you will find this when you draft and update or post.

- On LinkedIn you will find this when you use "create a post", the symbol appears on the bottom line.

- On Twitter, you will find the symbol under "what's happening" where you would create your tweet.

- On other platforms this function is usually part of your communication or story. On Instagram, look in "Your Story". If unsure use the help section of your chosen platform.

- When you create your poll, you can ask a question and set a number of alternative responses to gather opinion or feedback from your audience. Your network would be able to see scores on the voting, but not who has voted for which option.

- You can set the duration of your poll to make sure your target market has a chance to respond.

- On most sites there will be a "notifications" icon, these are a great way to ensure that you do not miss any activity from your network or discussion feeds.

Groups

You can use groups to start to network. All social media sites allow interaction between members and provide great networking opportunities.

- Discover groups by searching on key words or use the group icon to discover suggestions.

- Some groups are public, which means anyone can see what you contribute, some are private, only other group members can see what you post or share. Choose the privacy that works for your needs.

- Choose groups which have a relevance to your business. You might try local area groups, if you are targeting people regionally or national groups so you are not restricted to one geographic area. Join a few and see what people talk about and interact where you can.

- Look for groups of like-minded businesspeople, they may be great at sharing information, advice and also tips which may benefit you.

- You can share video clips, images, information, whatever you choose in these groups and your post will automatically appear at the top of your audiences feed or thread.

- Over time your posts will drop down the feeds as other network connections interact, so keep the comments and interactions live where you can.

- If anyone comments on your post, you will return to the top of the feed, so interaction is key to make sure you remain visible.

- Use your first post to introduce yourself to the group. Think about what you want to say, this should not be a sales pitch, but more about who you are, what you do and why you are in this group.

- You can and should follow up any leads from interactions with private messages, for example, via Facebook messenger or tools on other platforms to initiate more meaningful and warmer interactions.

- Think about starting your own group. Consider this carefully as you will have to administer the group, maybe act as a mediator, and ensure you are interacting in a timely manner.

4 Meetup and other dedicated contact sites

Meetup is a global tool that allow people to "meet up" physically or virtually. You can set up your own events, charge fees, attend others free and paid for meets/events and tap into an audience of over 58 million members.

Here are some tips to explore and utilise the site:

- Join Meetup for your country. Go to the website and follow the joining instructions. At this stage you can choose to join via other social media sites or use a separate email address. I would suggest using an email to sign in. Once verified you can access the site and build your profile.

- Upload a photo, help your audience recognise you and of course use that same professional image that you have on other platforms.

- Choose what you are interested in. A drop-down menu will appear choose as the option that best reflects what you want to use the site for.

- You will then see a menu of areas of interest, choose as many as you wish, the site will use these choices to start getting you connected to other groups of interest and of course allow you to create networking opportunities with like-minded people.

- Narrow down your interests on the next screen, then the site will present you with suggested groups to join.

- Start conversations in groups or message individuals from their profile pages.

- Become an Organiser and start your own groups and run online events.

- This is a monthly or 6 monthly paid service so explore what others are offering and think about how you might generate as an outcome from 'Organising'. Is it generating interest, new connections, monetising events, or other measures? Be clear on what you want to achieve before committing to this longer term and so you can evaluate if this is working for you.

There are other sites like Meetupout there that you can try.

Eventbrite

- Similar to Meetup used for hosting and registering for events. It is designed to bring people together with similar interests and again you can sell tickets to your events if you are a subscriber.

- Not always used for regular meetings, but it can bring people together.

Groupspaces

- Another option for group-coordination and event-planning.

- You can create a group, get members to sign up and collect information, add fees if desired, and create email lists to reach your network directly.

MEETin.org

- You will find Meetin.org on Facebook, they have migrated to this platform to socially network.

- Access this through your Facebook account, just search for Meetin.org and you can follow their page.

- This site is different as it is run as a free site, so no fees are applicable for its users. It is much more of a socially focused site than some of the others and not quite so active.

Citysocializer

- Again, more socially focused, but may allow access to networking again with local people and topics of interest. The site tries to encourage face to face networking where possible rather than some of the others which have really embraced the digital world.

As with everything on the internet, sites change, and new ones are added all the time. If you think these sites might be helpful to you do carry out some searches for sites to meet and feel free to try others that might catch your eye.

5   How can I utilise Zoom?

Zoom has grown in it use over the pandemic, but it can be used for much more than keeping in touch with the family! It is more of a meeting site than a site to build a network or audience on but can be great for hosting live meetings and events.

There are two levels of use of Zoom. Free which limits the time on calls to 45 mins when there are more than 3 attendees. Or Professional, which allows meetings which are not restricted by time or numbers of attendees.

- Join Zoom and create an account, then you can invite people to meetings, host events and start to interact.

- Consider the number of people you want to attend and if you need to upgrade to enable you to host more than 3 people.

- Get used to the technology! Find the camera button, know how to switch this on and off, the same with the mute function.

- Practice, practice, practice! Use the features such as polls to engage with the audience and canvas views, use the white board and see what you can do with the annotate tool to ensure that you are directing your viewers to the right information.

- Try out screen sharing and get used to how this feels and what to do if you share the wrong screen!

- Make sure your display name is correct! Do not use a Nickname or code, use your name and be authentic and present. You can rename yourself and if you are hosting can rename others in the participant list.

- You can share screens on the portal and others can share with you. You could share video, live documents, presentations and so on. Just look for the share screen button and you will see permissions in the extended menu.

- There is also a live chat function, so if anyone wants to ask questions or does not have audio connection they can still participate in your event or meeting.

- You can share links and documents in the chat so if you want to leave further information with attendees or direct them to other social media platforms you can.

- Use the waiting room feature so you physically accept people into the meeting rather than letting them auto join. This also allows you to check who is attending and welcome them in. Also, you can make sure you are ready to host and start on time.

- Ensure you have a good professional background when your camera is on. You can use effects to blur, use a virtual background or even a green screen to give that professional feel to your meeting.

- When you are ready to meet you can set up a meeting in your account, then copy the link and send this to all invited.

- Set passwords for events to prevent duplication of attendees or sharing of links.

- Get reports of attendance via the report section and use this to follow up with individuals post event.

- Record the event, make sure your attendees agree to this. When you activate recording, Zoom will announce that this has been enabled and that those who remain on the call are doing so with the knowledge of this.

- Share the recording with attendees if appropriate via an email link, you can also add other materials or links within this email to convey additional information or marketing.

- You can set up recurring meetings and these can be linked to your calendar, so you get reminders when meetings are about to start.

6   Teams and networking

Teams is a similar product to Zoom but owned by Microsoft. You may well have access to Teams already if you use Outlook.

Teams works in a similar way to Zoom so all the tips above will be valid for this platform too.

Here are some additional features that you might want to explore in teams:

- You can host instant or timed meetings via Teams and can meet with anyone who has access.

- You can join a Teams meeting anytime, from any device. Go to the meeting invite and select "Join Microsoft Teams Meeting". That will open a web page, where you'll see two choices: Download the Windows app or Join on the web instead.

- When you schedule a future meeting you can add a title, add email addresses of those you want to invite, choose the time, date, and duration. You can also add any pre-reading or documents you want to share in advance.

- Always use the description box in your invitations so that the attendees know what to expect.

- You can request responses to your meeting so you know who has accepted and you can allow or remove sharing of invitations. You might allow this for a free event where you want lots of attendees, restrict for a paid event where only the link holder can gain access.

- You can create a team of your own, have different members in different teams and share information via channels to them.

- A channel is a single place for a team to share messages, tools, and files.

I am sure you will agree, with the use of tools like Zoom and Teams you can really organise, hold, and facilitate some great meetings and create networking opportunities.

7 Online forums

Often if you are a Small Medium Enterprise business operator you normally don't have the luxury of big networks or trusted advisors to whom we can go to for advice and information. Everyone has their own specialist areas, skills and experience so forums can be a useful tool to go to for advice, business guidance, feedback, and even meet like-minded individuals or reach a target market.

The Internet is a great resource to find small business forums specifically aimed towards young entrepreneurs and business owners around the world. And with a wide range of industries and interests, you're sure to find a forum for almost any business-related topic—from business operations and financing to the latest technology and its use. So, in essence:

- An Online Forum is a web-based discussion site where people can hold conversations in the form of posted messages. Forums are made up of strings of discussions, a single conversation is called a "thread".

- Discussions are built up by users so that you can share information advice or hints and tips, depending on the nature of the forum. You may find that some forums can allow an individual to be anonymous and post, others will require you to sign up to the service and log in to post messages.

- Sometimes known as bulletin boards, you can discuss just about anything. It is worth reading the boards before you post to see the sort of discussion and type of person they attract.

- The easiest way to find forums is to carry out an internet search. Use a search engine to find "forums for (your topic)" and explore the results before you join.

Joining Sites

- Make sure you select the right sort of forum for you. Research the site by joining and starting to browse the discussions and level of the audience before jumping in and posting content.

- Before you start to post or contribute read and understand the rules for posting on each site. The rules may vary, and you don't want to be removed from the site or be banned for a silly mistake.

- Complete the registration form in full and use the email address that you have for your business, remember not to use a quirky nickname as your identity.

- View and make sure you understand the privacy controls of the forums you join.

- Never add your personal details within the posting. Keep your contact details safe and never disclose a home address, contact number or date of birth on the postings.

Here are some tips to help you use the discussion forums available:

- LinkedIn has its own discussion forums within the groups. You have to join the site to access these.

- Some groups are open networks where anyone can join, some are closed where you will need to demonstrate to the group's owner that you fit the qualifying criteria.

- Forum messages can then be viewed at any future time, even if you were not online when they were posted. Forums are a great way to foster interaction, discussion, and improve customer loyalty.

- There are a number of free forum sites, and some offer a hosting service to help manage your account.

- Use the forums actively. If you are simply promoting your organisation name, you may find you do not get many leads or contacts. If you actively answer other users' questions or add to posts you will soon become recognised amongst the forum members.

8 Using tools to automate SMS messages

- You can use Snapchat to send images to people. You can "friend" them via SMS message and if they accept you can then send them images as and when required.

- You can download apps from Google Play to manage automated SMS releases for you.

- SMS Scheduler one of these simple tools which you can programme to automatically release SMS messages choosing how often and the timing of their release.

- You can also use Tasker and AutoSMS, these too can be downloaded as Apps to your phone, and you can allow access to your contacts once installed.

- Many of these tools allow recipients to be typed in directly or selected from contacts and you can choose multiple recipients in one go.

- You chose how often, every 5 mins, every hour, daily, weekly, or monthly. The choice is yours to select what will support your marketing campaign or communication need.

- You can check the delivery status of each message and recipient so that you can see the target audience has been approached as scheduled.

- On an iPhone or other apple device, you can use Siri shortcuts - simply ask Siri about shortcuts to get a link to get the app on your apple product.

9 Skype

Increasingly organisations are considering using services like Skype as a means of contacting customers to resolve customer service queries.

For those not in the know, here is Wikipedia's definition of Skype

"The service allows users to communicate with peers by voice using a microphone, video by using a webcam, and instant messaging over the Internet. Phone calls may be placed to recipients on the traditional telephone networks. Calls to other users within the Skype service are free of charge, while calls to landline telephones and mobile phones are charged by opening an account. Skype has also become popular for its additional features, including file transfer, and videoconferencing."

There are competitors such as Zoom, Teams, Join.me, Google Hangouts, Facetime and Viber.

The main difference between these sites is cost and of course the functionality that you require.

- As your online organisation grows you can find your customer base growing internationally. Servicing customer queries which require you to speak to the customer can become expensive. Not so with Skype which is increasingly popular because it offers cheap calls to landlines in many countries.

- If, for example, you wish to speak to someone in Cape Town, South Africa, Skype uses the internet from your computer to connect to a local exchange in Cape Town at no cost to you. Then your connection to your customer is a local call at the call rates in that country.

- Skype gained its name as a means of no cost video calls between families living abroad, parents who are away from home phoning their children before they go to bed etc. Where you have a need to talk to a customer the Skype webcam facility provides this at no cost to either party.

- An option now is to subscribe to Skype for Business which has a range of packages with a monthly subscription. This gives you multi person video conferencing, screen sharing. So, if you have a disagreement with a customer over a signature for receipt of an order, you can show the customer that receipt from your computer.

10 Being prepared

Before you start networking understand what you want to gain from the experience, what content you want to present and how you want to be perceived.

100 + Top Tips For Social Media Success

Having a plan of attack can be useful for all of us, more so if you are not a natural networker.

- Understand your unique selling point and how to articulate it in a manner which is confident without being arrogant.

- Revisit your brand statement in chapter 1 to make sure this is still valid and to create that statement if you are not yet clear on what you want to say or be known for.

- Tell people what you talk about, use the features on site such as LinkedIn in Creator mode, use your Bios and profile pages. Post and share on these key topics and use the right hashtags on all social media to become associated with the content you consistently share.

- Know your audience. Do your research so that you present your information in a way to engage your audience.

- Look at attendee's social media sites. Get some knowledge of who will be at events and make a note to seek out those of most interest.

- Use their photos to help you recognise them at events!

- Find something in common to speak about, this might be their latest social media or blog post.

- Prepare some good questions, ones which demonstrate your knowledge as well as probing for content.

- Know what you want from each opportunity. Is it information or customers? Are you looking to deliver a raised perception of your level of expertise or to convince your audience that you are the one for them?

- Make notes from any networking opportunities. Make sure you follow up on leads and let your contact know how you get on. Keep in touch, keep them informed and thank them for any success they help to generate.

Chapter 8 - Top 10 tips for avoiding traps

1 Security

There are many people on the internet who scam others, steal identities or are phishing for information to name a few. You need to understand some basic ways to protect yourself. This is not an exhaustive list, research your security needs and choose what is right for your business.

Internet

- If using your home to run your business, make sure that your server is safe. When using an internet connection (wired or wireless) you need to make sure you have a password active to prevent others from tapping into your network.

- Change the default password for your wireless connection regularly as they are usually easy for hackers to access.

- Make sure you install and maintain anti-virus software. You can buy protection from most PC suppliers and over the internet. As viruses are released daily you must ensure that once you install the software you update it least once a week and run regular scans.

- Scan any documents you are sent in case they have a virus embedded within their content.

- Check your provider's website to see of any updates to the software are available. Your provider may set up an automatic update prompt.

- When you register with a site sometimes you are offered the option to sign in via Facebook or Google – always use your own details to sign in. If this site was hacked, they could access your personal data on the other platforms.

Emails

- Emails are the most common source of viruses and malware. Beware the "once in a lifetime offer" with a link even if it is from a known individual.

- Never open emails from an unknown source without first scanning with your security. Most software will scan all incoming emails and push them to spam or alert as suspicious. If not proceed with caution.

- Often poor grammar or spelling mistakes highlight the possibility of a rogue email.

- Banks don't email you with "issues" on your account. Always contact the bank directly and report any untoward contact.

- Never sign in via these emails as again these are often scams.

- Never provide your bank details and password (which they will then capture).

- Never contact them via a premium number which will cost a small fortune.

- Viruses are carried in attachments, if suspicious contact the originator of the email to validate the information before opening and infecting your network.

Passwords

- When setting personal passwords never choose your own name or a word which can easily be associated with you.

- Think of the line in a poem or song that you remember easily, then use the first letter of each word. You could also add a few numbers.

- Check an old password on howsecureismypassword.com to find out how quickly, with today's technology, a hacker could gain access to your information.

- Use different passwords – if a hacker obtains one, they will try it on all the sites that they have discovered you are using.

- Log sites and passwords in a password protected document.

- If you have a hard copy list of passwords, file this in a non-descript book on a shelf, not near your computer or laptop. If you are burgled, you may lose your equipment but at least you have all your passwords and can then change them quickly.

- If you use an iPhone or iPad you can check if passwords have been compromised. Go to your settings, choose passwords, verifying your account (face ID, fingerprint etc) then choose security recommendations. This will show you the "at risk" passwords and sites to take action on.

- You will also have this function on most Android devices, just Google search the how to check and follow the guidance online.

Site etiquette

- Know where you have uploaded your information, added profiles, focus documents or CV so that you can easily update or remove them.

- Get to know each site's security settings, their function and the etiquette of the site..

- Review and understand the Terms & Conditions before ticking the box.

- Know who will have access to or visibility of your information, files and images. You may still own the copyright, but the site may specify that they can use the items without telling you.

- Understand admin rights, who should be granted access and why.

- Set up a dummy email account to use to first register on new sites. Once you are happy to use the site then you can change back to your personal email account. This will reduce the potential for spam and heavy marketing campaigns from an unwanted site.

- Google search your name to see what everyone else can see about you.

- If you use your mobile for business, you might also consider purchasing anti-malware and an anti-virus package for this too.

2 Data compliance requirements

The Data Protection Act 2018 controls how your personal information is used by organisations, businesses or the Government. The Data Protection Act 2018 is the UK's implementation of the General Data Protection Regulation (GDPR).

After leaving the EU on January 1, 2021, the UK is officially not a part of the EU's GDPR any longer, i.e., the EU's GDPR does not have any domestic jurisdiction in the UK as it had from May 2018. The UK has passed its own version called the UK-GDPR, which alongside the Data Protection Act of 2018, is in effect now. Access accurate information via the UK Government website.

www.gov.uk/government/publications/guide-to-the-general-data-protection-regulation

Everyone responsible for using personal data has to follow strict rules called "data protection principles". They must make sure the information is:

- Used fairly, lawfully and transparently.

- Used for specified, explicit purposes.

- Used in a way that is adequate, relevant and limited to only what is necessary.

- Accurate and, where necessary, kept up to date.

- Kept for no longer than is necessary.

- Handled in a way that ensures appropriate security, including protection against unlawful or unauthorised processing, access, loss, destruction or damage.

There is stronger legal protection for more sensitive information, such as:

- Race, ethnic background, political opinions, religious beliefs, trade union membership, genetics, biometrics (where used for identification), health, sex life or orientation.

There are separate safeguards for personal data relating to criminal convictions and offences.

Your rights as an individual

Under the Data Protection Act 2018, you have the right to find out what information the Government and other organisations store about you. These include the right to:

- Be informed about how your data is being used.

- Access personal data.

- Have incorrect data updated.

- Have data erased.

- Stop or restrict the processing of your data.

- Data portability (allowing you to get and reuse your data for different services).

- Object to how your data is processed in certain circumstances.

You also have rights when an organisation is using your personal data for:

- Automated decision-making processes (without human involvement).

- Profiling, for example to predict your behaviour or interests.

3 Scams and hoaxes

The internet is a huge melting pot of information and people and people who play with the truth! Anything which appears too good to be true is probably just that, don't get tempted. The selection is vast, some areas to watch out for are:

- Jobs which don't exist.

- Suggestions that you are the beneficiary of a large estate.

- People asking for money to get them home from disasters.

- Emails from a friend's account stating special offers on link xxxx.

- Messages prompting you to look at a video you are featured in.

- The pyramid scheme offering you a fortune in return for a small financial investment.

- Click here to win XYZ – you win a wonderful virus or let the hacker in to your email address book.

There is always the concern of identity theft and also the potential for spam when you are researching sites to use. Instead of using your own personal email create a new one. In fact, create two.

- One which is totally unrelated to you it could just be a combination of letters and numbers. You use this email when you are first registering on a site.

- Once you decide you want to continue with the site you can change it to your preferred address. This will mean any spam will go into this 'rubbish' email account and the account can either be ignored or deleted once your research is complete.

- Email address two is one which is more organisation focussed. It may be related to your own domain name, or if you are not having a website you create it so that all your organisation related communication is now in one place. Helping to avoid you missing an organisation related email amongst your personal details.

4 Time management, efficiency and costs

There is always a cost for using the internet and social media. The main cost is your time and your data/information. The more sites you visit the more 'cookies' or trails you leave and this is valuable data for marketing. Most sites make their money by allowing companies and individuals to buy access to your data directly through them.

- Make sure you read any Terms and Conditions before you click the accept box. Know where and how your information is going to be used.

- Many sites will have 'free' use. This is generally where you provide information or data and the site is then able to make that information public and sell on your content to other users.

- Some sites will offer premium services. Always explore the free options first and only upgrade when there are functions you find you need but cannot access for free.

- Be careful when using your phone abroad. Not only will you incur costs for both making and receiving calls and text messages, you could also be charged for roaming data. This is really important if all of your emails are sent to your device as if you access these outside of a wireless network you will incur download charges.

- Check with your mobile provider before you travel and see what you need to do to deactivate services or buy a "bundle" before you go to minimise the risk of expensive bills.

- Make sure if you have a contracted mobile phone that the plan you have chosen provides enough download for all of the data and internet use you may need. The hidden costs in phone contracts can be huge if you consume your allowance then have to pay for any additional usage.

- Most phone providers will allow you to view your usage on their websites and manage you bills so do keep an eye on what you have used and adjust your plan if needs be.

- Always set up your renewable accounts on an automatic basis. You will be advised in advance that your contract is up for renewal.

- If you want to renew you don't need to do anything the money will be taken from your account – credit card, PayPal automatically. If you decide you don't want to continue the contract you let them know.

- This will ensure that your domain name, for example, will be protected as yours until you decide that you don't want it anymore.

- If you opt for the invoice prior to payment, it is very easy to forget and once your brand is up and going your domain name can be extremely valuable.

- It has been known that an individual was on the invoice prior to payment agreement, forgot to pay and their domain name was then available for anyone to take. The individual was then contacted by a company offering their domain back for £10K. Not a good experience.

Consider the time you take for your online activity balanced with the benefits.

- Think about where you want to put your content. Consider the time it takes to post and update. Research your competition, investigate best practice, and understand the return on investment for your time as well as any ancillary charges.

- What will happen if you get into a volume of conversations on LinkedIn, Facebook and Twitter? Will you have the time to manage this?

- Will your target audience benefit or be turned off by your excessive 'conversations'?

5 Passive vs proactive

If you just sit back and wait for new customers or business, you might be waiting a very long time!

- Most sites will increase your visibility the more that you use them. Pushing you higher up in the search results.

- Make sure that you update information regularly on all sites to keep the pages fresh.

- Think about adding photos, video and other media to keep the site interesting.

- Encourage re-tweeting and liking your posts on any site you use.

- Search engine optimisation monitors visits and use of your sites so you need to actively manage your online presence.

6   Keeping up to date

The problem with the internet is that it is a constantly changing feast with content, presentation and trends moving sometimes on a daily basis. You can be on a site one day and the next it looks different.

There is nothing you can do to stem this flow of change and, to be fair, why you would want to. Consider the changes as opportunities but do also make sure you are safe.

- If you are advised that there are going to be changes to a site's settings use this as a prompt to go in and check that all your settings are still in place and that you understand the new ones.

- Sign up for news from various sites to ensure you are aware of the changes. Socialmediaexaminer.com is a site where you are able to register and get emails letting you know the forthcoming changes and impact on social media and SEO for example when Google changes its algorithms.

- Technology changes regularly so make sure your website is up to date. There are sites you can register with to check your site out for compliance and errors.

- Keep up to date with scheduled personal training sessions. There are many opportunities to learn for free including the OU, various universities, BBC and courses via aggregators such as 'Alison' and 'Coursera'. Not all the courses have recognised certificates, but if you are looking for information the free option may be useful.

- Sign up to get advice from the professional bodies pertinent to your industry.

7   Closing accounts

Your business may change, your time available or your budget may reduce so understand how to close accounts if you need to.

- Facebook -while you're logged in, go to your settings and click the "Delete My Account" button. It may take up to 14 days before your profile is completely gone. Doing it this way deletes all of your data, and it cannot be reactivated.

- Twitter – go to your account settings page, click "Deactivate my account" at the bottom. Your account is deleted completely, but it will take a few weeks before results stop showing up in searches.

- LinkedIn – go to your settings page; click the "Account" icon, then the "close your account" link.

- If you have forgotten accounts: accountkiller.com will give you direct links to delete accounts from more than 500 sites.

- There are many sites which allow you to find addresses, phone numbers, and assorted data. Search for the options and then check the reviews prior to using them.

- Ghostery is one of a number of sites which block ads and trackers from when you look at websites. There is a free and a paid option.

8   Customer focus

The old statement "all things to all people" is often the total opposite of what you should consider when you go online. Customer-focused businesses are built around customers' needs. Becoming one involves concentrating on how every interaction helps the customer, rather than how it helps your business.

- Understand what your customer wants from your business by asking for feedback, suggestions and recommendations.

- Respond to customers in a timely manner, even if it is an auto response email outlining when you will take action, at least the customer knows their message has arrived and when to expect a reply.

- Keep your promises. There is nothing worse than expectation which is not delivered.

- If something has gone wrong for your customer, manage the relationship carefully. Defuse their complaint by taking their information efficiently, ask relevant questions and repeat back to them so that they know that you have all the appropriate facts. Tell them what you are going to do about it and make sure that you act accordingly. Once resolved, check back with them to confirm that it has been completed satisfactorily. If complaints are managed professionally, the complainant often becomes one of your most loyal customers.

9 Brand protection, business idea, copyright

A brand is "an intangible marketing or business concept that helps people identify a company, product, or individual." Your logo, slogans, or other identifying marks are marketing tools that help promote goods and services. New and good products attract counterfeiters. Not having brand protection puts your brand at the danger of losing all your time and money invested in your brand.

There is no real way to protect your business idea prior to launch other than getting anyone you share information with to enter into a non-disclosure agreement (NDA).

- Before you do a lot of work on logos and registration, do your research on your proposed business name and design factors like colours and style. If your ideas, designs, style and colours are too close to another company you may find a legal claim against you.

- If you want to protect your brand identity you have to register a trademark for your company name, logos, and slogans. By using the trademark symbol, you notify other people that specific products are your property.

- There's no legal requirement that forces you to trademark your business or brand name (logo). You can have what are known as 'common law' rights to your business name without formally registering it.

- If you decide to register your trademark, you'll be able to take legal action against anyone who uses your brand without your permission, including counterfeiters.

- The trademark symbol (TM) is a mark that companies often use on a logo, name, phrase, word, or design that represents the business. However, the (TM) symbol has no legal meaning which means you can use the symbol on any mark that your company uses without registering it.

- The easiest way to correctly register your logo is to do it online with the Intellectual Property Office (IPO). As this is a legal agreement, it can be beneficial to seek advice from a specialised lawyer, especially if you are registering a community trademark.

Copyright protects your work and stops others from using it without your permission. There isn't a register of copyright works in the UK. You automatically get copyright protection when you create original literary, dramatic, musical and artistic work, including illustration and photography. Copyright law lays out a framework of rules around how that work can be used. It sets out the rights of the owner, as well as the responsibilities of other people who want to use the work.

- What happens if you break copyright law? Depending on the severity of the infringement, the result can be a fine or even imprisonment. If found guilty of copyright infringement in a magistrate's court, your business could be fined up to £50,000 and you could face a jail term of up to six months.

- Change your username and email address to one that doesn't connect people to you personally and use this if you want to continue access to blogs or forums that are not aligned to your future career.

10 Quality vs Quantity

Whatever your business, the quality of your products and services differentiates you from your competition as does your online content. It's very easy to be tempted to shout about your business on every social media platform available, this may be very costly in time and also in the impression you are giving to your true customers.

- Don't keep adding to your offering just to fill gaps, understand why you need to add more and what value it gives to your customer base balanced with how it will affect your business, its budget and efficiency.

- Fake followers are a real problem for any business and many businesses are often seen with fake followers on Instagram and other social media channels just to keep up the number of viewers on their website. Once your true customers start questioning the validity of your numbers, they lose trust in your business.

- There is pressure for you to be available and represented on a multitude of platforms at all times. You need to select the number of social media sites which are manageable for your business, whilst also making sure they are the right places to promote your business.

- The approach to your website needs to be well thought out and easy to use. Too much information or slow loading does not appeal to the short attention spans of most people today.

- The use of smart phones for all aspects of online business means that your content needs to be accessible and clearly presented.

Chapter 9 - Top 10 tips for going live

When we are about to "go live" into the world of advertising, social media and marketing we need to make sure we are fully prepared and ready to launch our offer.

Your first approach to your market needs to be memorable, make an impact for the right reasons, and deliver the professional brand and image you strive to create.

Throughout this book you will find different elements to get you to this point. Now is the time to check the aspect you need to go live. There are questioned listed under the key areas and a checklist for easy documentation at the end.

1   Content

Does all the content you have prepared promote you or your business appropriately.

- What is it that you can offer your clients?
- What are the benefits for your target market?
- What is your unique selling point?
- Why should your client choose you instead of your competition?
- When and how often should you post on your channels and website?
- Have you researched the right analytical tools to measure your success?
- Have you all the software tools you need?
- Are you well practiced and confident in sharing your content online?
- Is your content useful, informative, timely, appropriate?
- Have you got enough content prepared for your schedule?

2   Equipment

Chapter 2 covered the details around the equipment and software you should investigate and by now you should have made your choices and be proficient in getting the best out of your chosen kit. Here are some suggestions to make sure you are prepared.

Have you got all the hardware you need? This includes:

- PC or Laptop with sufficient RAM and storage
- External storage devices

- Smart phone
- Shredder

Internet access that is reliable and has sufficient speed and capacity.

Office space, either owned or rented.

General office supplies, chair, desk and lockable storage for hard copy documents if necessary.

Paper supplies - stationery, business cards, headed paper, invoices, flyers.

3   Software

Does your software cover all aspects required for your business?

- Accounting
- Order processing
- Security
- Secure customer data management
- Analytical tools
- Can it be upgraded if your business expands?

Do you understand how to use it, or do you have someone who will be managing it for you?

For social media specific software, you might want to investigate programmes that help to:

- Automate posts across various platforms.
- Track success and provide meaningful statistics.
- Allow collaboration of users to post and share under one company.

4   Contributors, Collaborators, and Contracts

You may want to find others to help with your content creation or management of your website or social media pages, have you clear instructions on:

- What they need to do and the style to project.
- How they will be measured.
- Contracts, fees and payment details.

So where can you find contributors and collaborators?

- You could consider using Students who are studying in your field to write articles or contribute papers for you to feature. This gives something to you and something that they can use to showcase or support their studies.

- Sites such as Mypocketskill might be a useful starting point to discover who can help you.

- You could feature a Guest Writer or Blogger, identify the posts, articles, blogs or vlogs that have a great interaction and people who have a high number of followers to ensure that you are working with someone who is already promoting their work.

- Approach these people and see if they would like to be featured or if they write articles for others. At the very least it is a great networking opportunity.

- Cross-promote, if someone already has several hundred or more followers, if they feature the fact that they are writing on your sites with a signpost (URL) to them this will boost your viewers.

- If you want to write posts for others or find the most recent guest posts for your profession, try a simple Google search – Keyword "guest post" replace the keyword with what you are looking for i.e. Logistics "guest post".

- Take a look at the site myblogguest to see blogs about guest blogging and how to get involved or find others to contribute.

- Take a look at freelance sites, Fiverr, Freelancer, Upwork and so on may help. These will be of course paid services, but a clear plan of what you are paying for will be included as part of the service via these sites.

- Who is writing for you competitors? Take a look at their sites, chances are that these authors would be willing to write for you too.

5   Contracts

A contract with third party to protect yourself and also the guest writer could be via a Legal professional or sometimes you may have access to legal documents as part of an insurance you have purchased.

Look at sites offering guest writer or contributor positions sometimes they list contract information or Terms and

Conditions (T&Cs). Even so please do make sure you take advice to make sure you are fully protected in the event of any claims against you.

At a basic level check any agreements include:

- Information about originality.

- There is no plagiarism or copyright infringements in the work submitted.

- Do you want to allow affiliate links or marketing?

- Any conditions around citing sources or using quotes.

- Content and images submitted are royalty free.

This is not intended to be the basis of a legal contract, simply a quick guide to get you thinking of what you may need to consider if choosing to use others content or contributions.

6 Costs

When going live, it is easy to get caught up in the moment and forget that your business is incurring cost as it runs. To avoid hitting cash flow problems, we need to keep a very close eye on planned and unplanned expenses!

In general, the most common costs you will face when going live will have already been planned and accounted for in your budget. But here is a quick checklist to make sure that you have indeed acted in these areas and of course you plan to monitor them.

- Fees due/payable for research undertaken.

- Any borrowing from Banks or other lenders.

- Start up and ongoing equipment needs.

- Insurances, licences and any other certifications.

- Training fees and subscriptions.

- Technology fees, software purchase and associated support packages.

- Legal fees and Accountancy / accounting packages or software.

- Marketing expenditure.

7   Revenue and Banking Details

Ensure you are able to make and receive payments in your business name and that you have a planned invoicing schedule and clear payment information.

- Lay out your payment terms clearly in any contracts and restate them on any invoices generated.

- Use an accounting system to generate automated billing and monitor the dates invoices are due to be raised and sent to clients.

- Use an accountant or if you are going to manage this manually you will need to set up your own systems for remembering to bill, acknowledge receipt and chase late payers.

- Consider payment in advance for your services. This is commonplace with some types of services when booking via the internet.

- If your business is not a pay in advance type of service, consider deposits or cancellation fees, clearly outlined within the booking process or contracts.

- Include payment details on the invoice, account number, sort code, name etc.

- Make sure you are not only tracking the invoice generation but also tracking the payments received.

- Check your bank is set up correctly for invoicing, all types of payments (cards, mobile wallets etc) and charges are understood.

8   Scheduling

Scheduling is essential for social media, invoices, payments, renewals and so on. Here is a checklist of the key things to schedule to help. This is not intended to be a comprehensive list, so space has been left for you to add areas of focus for your business.

Area	Provider / Partner	Cost / Commitment	Review Date
Accountant			
Additional Branding costs			
Advertising			

Advertising spend			
Affiliate marketing			
Auto Messaging tools			
Bank account costs			
Banking			
Bookkeeper			
Business email			
Business insurances			
Cash management			
Communications			
Courses			
Credit management fees			
Data compliance			
Data management			
Design fees and ongoing support			
Domain Name fees			
Equipment Loan or Hire			
Fees for content creation			
Fees for Promotional sites (Groupon etc)			
Hosting costs			
Insurances			

100 + Top Tips For Social Media Success

Legal advice			
Logo design			
Mail services			
Mobile contracts			
Networking group memberships			
Personal insurances			
Premium subscriptions			
Premium Web Meeting services (Zoom etc)			
Professional body membership renewals			
Professional development			
Publishing Licences (e.g. Microsoft Office)			
Scheduling tools			
Social media			
Software licences			
Tech support packages			
Technology			
Third party payment providers			
Third party services			
Web analytics			
Website updates			
Website fees			

9 Legal requirements, accessibility, data protection

There are several areas where you will need to investigate to ensure to do things correctly. The phrase "ignorance is no defense" echoes strongly across the internet. If you break the law, you are still liable even if you have no knowledge of the law being broken. Do research and get legal advice when you don't understand.

Much of the detail of this section is covered in Chapters 1 and 5. Please refer to these chapters for more information. But here is a summary of the key points to review prior to launch:

- Understand your legal requirements and ensure you adhere to them – content information, accessibility, email campaigns, data protection and storage.

- Use online resources and the regulatory bodies or lead bodies for your industry or sector to look at latest compliance requirements.

Check that you have covered or considered the following points:

- Are you compliant with the latest GDPR regulations?

- Have you included "unsubscribe" functions with your email and "stop" for SMS campaigns?

- Are your Terms and Conditions clearly outlined on your website and other platforms?

- Have you included disclaimers where appropriate or needed?

- Copyright rules – are you aware of these and included the © as required on your materials?

- Distance selling regulations – have you reviewed these and are you compliant?

- Is your website accessible to all? Have you considered the use of colours, screen reader compatibility, fonts etc?

Review Chapter 2 to refresh your understanding, this simple check is simply designed to get you thinking have you covered what you need to.

10 Analysis

Once you go live check progress regularly against your marketing plan.

100 + Top Tips For Social Media Success

To be able to measure and report on the return on investment, you need to have a plan just like you have a plan for posting.

Measuring the ROI (return on investment) on your social media activities helps justify what you are doing and where you should focus in the future. There is more on this in chapter 10 - Managing Progress.

You need to measure components such as:

- Reach – How many people saw your post?

- Site Traffic – How many users clicked through to your website or landing page as a result of your post?

- Leads Generated – Who filled out a landing page form or asked for additional information?

- Conversions – How many people downloaded an offer or coupon, signed up for your newsletter or converted on some other action?

- Revenue Generated – How much money resulted from the specific campaign?

Check your visits with various analytical tools

You can use UTM (Urchin Tracking Model) codes to help track visits from one site to another.

UTM codes are basically a short code you can add to a URL or link to see where traffic comes from to land on that page and also gives other statistics.

Google has a UTM generator that you can use and add in the parameters you want to track, such as what sites the traffic came from, the campaign it relates to. i.e., discount codes, seasonal campaigns.

You need to track your metrics and then act on the data collected.

- Decide which elements are working and which are not.

- Review the less successful areas and amend to give more positive results.

- Review and amend again only if you believe it will be of benefit.

- Remember that the social media population is not static and you have to stay on top of the correct market for your business.

- Manage the time you are prepared to invest in posting

Remember most sites will have their own base line metrics you can tap into. If you use scheduling tools these will give you more information. Decide if you need deeper statistics and analysis following this initial launch period then maybe investigate providers and or tools to use.

Chapter 10 - Top 10 Tips for managing progress

Whatever you do, you need to understand how your organisation is progressing. To do this successfully you need to plan what, how and when you are going to measure and compare results generated from any campaign. The following chapter looks at key tips to really see how successful you have been and more importantly could be.

It's best to think, "If I can't measure it... Don't do it!!"

1   Tracking Progress

It is important to track your progress to really understand the benefits from your investment. Many tools are available free on the internet, some you do have to pay for. It is worth exploring the results that the free sites give you and if you need more then investigate what you get for your money if you upgrade or use subscription tools.

- Track not only the results that you get but the time spent on activity.

- A simple way to track uplift is to take a note of the number of followers, subscribers, or contacts you have now on social media sites, by platform. Get active and monitor over a fixed period, say 1 month, then measure again. You hopefully will see an uplift in the figures.

For site specific tracking try these tools:

- Facebook, use Insights, go to pages and on the side menu, choose "Insights". This will show information such as page followers, engagement, views and page likes, and more. If you have an administrator for your business page, they can see these analytics too.

- LinkedIn, for free you can see analytics by post. Go to "views of your post" and you will see by date the statistics. You can also see who viewed your profile and see who is viewing with associated statistics and users.

- Instagram, this is really the same process as Facebook, simply open the app, navigate to your profile and tap on the three bars in the upper right corner. Access insights and tap on the graph tool.

For websites, you may well have analytics included in any package you agree with a web designer or on the platforms themselves. If not, you can use Google Analytics, Google PageSpeed, Wooranks and many others. Some are free to use others you will need to pay for. Some sites will monitor traffic etc, others page availability. Think about how important your website is and what might happen if the site is down for any length of time. Do you have support available for a quick recovery if needs be? If not, you may need to build in contingency to allow for this.

2   Advertising Results

As part of your marketing strategy, you really need to have established what results you expected to achieve by using advertising.

You need to understand what you want to achieve, sales uplift, generate interest and enquiries or build your company image/branding.

You may have a limited budget to use for advertising so you really need to make sure that you use the right media for you and that it works.

- Use online tools such as Google Analytics to see how much interest is generated from your marketing.

- Pinterest has a tools such as Cyfy, Google Reader and Pinerly associated with it to help you see what is driving interest.

- Use Statigram to analyse Instagram traffic.

- For Facebook use Facebook Insights.

- IceRocket can help you monitor the web looking at blogs, Twitter, and Facebook, and provides results in a one page easy to read document.

- To identify influencers, Klout will highlight the key people in your network that could help position your organisation or product and show you how you rate on the web.

3   Marketing Plan V Budget

Understanding of the effectiveness of your website and social media usage will ensure that your costs are benefitting your business therefore, your return on investment. Create achievable targets to measure against and understand your ROI.

What is ROI?

- ROI can be defined as: 'A performance measure used to evaluate the efficiency of an investment or to compare the efficiency of a number of different investments'.

- To calculate ROI, the benefit (return) of an investment is divided by the cost of the investment; the result is expressed as a percentage or a ratio."

source - www.investopedia.com

ROI = (Revenue generated from campaign – Cost of the Campaign)

Cost of Marketing Campaign

Money

- Analyse what income your spend is generating and monitor the monetary value to best utilise your investment.

- If you find that a certain campaign is generating a higher ROI than others, you can apply more of your budget to that campaign.

- Use a spread sheet. Regularly track generated income, days remaining in the campaign and KPIs set. This will give you a good indication of how things are progressing.

Time

You need to invest your time in the media that is working for your audience so you will need to utilise analytical information from these sites. Use Google Analytics or other tools to define these statistics for you.

- Measure the hit rate of your website and see if enough consumers are looking.

- Monitor time spent on your page, conversions to sales or enquiries, if they move through your site.

- Consider time spent on planning and executing the marketing campaigns you have chosen. If you are spending 70 hours per week and only generating £220 profit, that's a very poor hourly return.

- Use feedback mechanisms such as, 'contact us', 'like our page', 'pop up feedback' requests.

Make sure you diarise review meetings to focus on what advertising and marketing is delivering for you.

4   Feedback

Feedback is essential for any organisation to understand how your customers and clients value your service so you are able to deliver what they want.

- If your feedback is not so good this is doubly valuable as this provides information on where you need to improve or change the service you offer.

- You could use surveys from companies such as SurveyMonkey, Microsoft Forms and other providers.

- Consider using QR codes to drive traffic to your surveys and forms.

- Use Polls on social media sites, again as the questions that matter, make the survey private so others can see only their answers not those of others.

- Make sure you have a contact us button and a feedback button on your website, it is monitored and replies sent.

- If you have a complex complaint to manage, make sure you acknowledge the customer quickly, explain a timeline for updates and keep them informed.

- Monitor your social media feeds carefully. Make sure you have alerts on that will notify you if you are mentioned, but also keep an eye on the chat feeds and again make sure you are responsive to any issues.

5   Monitoring Social Media sites

LinkedIn

LinkedIn contains areas within your profile to get written recommendations from your clients, customers, and network colleagues.

- Recommendations can only come from a current level one connection. You may need to target certain people to network with before you approach them on LinkedIn.

- Add a link for feedback to your promotional materials, websites, Twitter or Facebook pages, to 'recommend me on LinkedIn'. Make sure to include your personalised URL so that they recommend the right person!

- You may need to ask for recommendations so start with those who know you best. As more recommendations come in, you can choose which ones to show or hide by editing your profile, selecting recommendations, and then following the steps online to manage the recommendations you have received.

- LinkedIn 'endorsements' relate to the skills you add to your LinkedIn profile. Adding in skills and strengths will allow your network to click on the skill and show that they rate you for this helping build your overall reputation.

Facebook and Instagram

- On Facebook get people to leave comments or "like" your page. Comments are more meaningful so try to encourage users to leave them wherever possible.

- On Instagram people can "like" your photos so make sure that you are updating your site frequently and give your followers something to comment on.

- Monitor the images that get the most attention and response for your market and do more of this. Keep a note of the numbers for each type of image and the comments that your viewers add.

Twitter

- Encourage your audience to tweet about you. A prompt on your website or a message to all your followers might encourage them to support you.

- Remember to include a # (topic) so that all tweets find their way onto an amalgamated search result.

- Consider re-tweeting positive feedback to highlight what you do and how professional you are.

- There are lots of software providers out there that have created tools to help you monitor Twitter feeds and respond in the same area.

6   Monitoring Selling sites

Groupon, eBay and other e-tailers

- If promoting offers via Groupon or groups in LinkedIn, make sure that you capture the email addresses of all interested parties.

- This will allow you to request to link with them once they have used the offer and encourage them to leave feedback accordingly.

- A seller's reputation on eBay is critical. Follow up any missing feedback and investigate any buyer issues before they leave feedback. Make sure this is clear on your advert to offer direct customer service before feedback is left.

- When using eBay make sure that if you purchase items and make sure that you leave feedback for your seller.

- It is vital that you act on any negative feedback left and that potential customers can see what you have done to resolve any potential disputes or issues to a positive outcome.

7   Monitoring Blogs, Vlogs and Podcasts

Blog guidelines indicate that titles, headlines, subheaders or body text which should flow into the copy naturally. Be careful on content, would you say it to someone? If not, don't write it in your blog.

Vlogging laws can vary, for most countries, you are allowed to film in a public place but not allowed to film people in a place where they can expect privacy and if asked to stop, you do.

Podcast disclaimers should include a statement around the primary purpose of the podcast being to educate. It should state that the podcast does not constitute advice or services.

8   Monitoring your Website

Analyse common questions that are being asked about your product or services. Can you make any content or information clearer or more useful?

Is the contact us area being used? Respond to any comments promptly, both positive and negative.

Put into place a customer service standard and maintain it.

9   Measuring Success

This is where statistics relating to search engine optimisation, view of images, pages and other social media interactions should be measured. Who is looking at you/your services and why?

First you need to identify what metrics matter to you the most to achieve your business goal.

Then look at the platforms you're currently on, not all social networks have the same metrics available from within the platform.

When you have your metrics listed you need to check them against your business needs. Some may be primary and some secondary. Focus on the former and be selective about secondary metrics. Here are some suggestions.

LinkedIn

- Use the "who's viewed my profile" link to see who is looking at you. You might consider upgrading to see a full 90 days-worth of these statistics and see why you are being found.

Twitter

- Check who your followers are. Do they re-tweet what you put out there?

Facebook

- Use Facebook Insights at least once a month to see how your page is performing, how many "likes" you have, who is following you and where the most activity is being generated from.

- Remember to compare this to your KPIs and targets set in your marketing plan.

Instagram

- You can use Statigram to see what images people like that you share. Use this to do more of what they like and build up your following.

Blogs, Vlogs and Podcasts

- Who is reading your blog? Is the "following" rate going up or down? Think about planning regular interesting new content and use the tools available to help you to automate the process. Consider Hootsuite, Bufferapp etc.

- Similar to blogs, how big is your audience for your vlogs or podcasts.

Websites

- Tools such as Google Analytics will help you to see how successful your web site is in the monitoring of certain functions. For example, the total number of visits, new visitors and returning visitors, unique visitors, average time per site, average pages viewed per visit.

- Consider using Google AdWords to track the words to use in your site and how they drive traffic.

Once you have measured activity, your next step is to analyse the output. This will help you to plan any changes to your processes or approach to your use of social media and the internet when promoting your business.

10 Managing Quality

Quality of service needs to be measured across all areas.

- This might be speed of order completion, customer feedback, or marketing metrics. All of these areas should be monitored to help you establish if you are indeed giving the customers what they want and expect.

Customer satisfaction, performance, and Complaints

- Customer service can be measured with simple feedback tools. The idea is to use some very specific questions that relate to the goals you have set yourself.

- It is important to decide what you are measuring as part of your planning otherwise you cannot devise tools to ensure you track and act on the feedback generated.

- Use a questionnaire on your website, send automated feedback texts, sample customers with direct mails or calls to really discover what they think of your services.

- Be prepared for positive and negative feedback! If you receive feedback that you feel is unjust, ask a few more client/customers about this area. If it is just a one off, don't be too concerned, if there is an emerging theme, act on it as quickly as possible.

- If you have any negative feedback, address it immediately with a response directly to the complainant.

- Ask them once resolved to share how well the issue has been dealt with. People are far more likely to share negative service experiences, and we want to make the most of the positive actions.

- Make sure you monitor your social media feeds.

- If your organisation provides any form of service make sure you check TripAdvisor.

- Here like Twitter, people can say anything they like about your services, and it is automatically added to your page. Act swiftly to resolve issues as more and more of your potential clients will check reviews before booking your services.

- Lots of people like to rant about poor service on blogs. Run a Google blog search daily to make sure you keep up with all internet postings from your community.

There are many tools now available to help us manage quality. Here are some ways you can tap into these areas to help you:

- If you use telephone systems to communicate with customers, speech recognition programmes can analyse and record calls. You can often get analysis of their findings such as common issues, words and so on that could help pinpoint issues.

- The same sort of service can look at Text analysis, so if you are communicating in the written format via text messages, emails, WhatsApp, or other applications this could be a good, automated way of identifying themes.

There are some more personal approaches to understanding the quality provided that you could consider:

- Maybe use a "mystery shopper" to review your services. This could be via call, social media interaction or in person, whatever may work for your business or company.

- Ask your customers, make calls, make it personal to see how they found your company. Often, we only hear from customers that have had a poor experience, make those feel valued even if they have experienced great quality. Make them feel valued and they will return.

Qualitative data and word clouds

Qualitative data is hard to analyse so Word Clouds give you a way to visualise text at a glance giving you a view of the words used and their frequency. They can be used for speedy analysis, the larger the word, the more often it's been used. There are many free word cloud generators e.g. monkeylearn.com, freewordcloudgenerator.com

Using word clouds for analysis gives many benefits.

- Quick and easy for large volumes of qualitative data.

- Recognise patterns in data to show opinions and used in sentiment analysis. To determine positive, negative or neutral comments.

- Assists monitoring your brand or product and understanding your customer needs.

To create a word cloud you type, paste or upload text into a word cloud generator, customise your word cloud. Simply:

- Collect your data.

- Input into a word cloud generator. Usually, Copy/Paste or uploading a .CSV file.

- Remove filler and non-essential words: the, is, and etc.

- Select your font and colours.

- Choose how many words will be displayed.

- Click the button to generate your Word Cloud!

You can also use Word Clouds on your website to show people what you are focusing on.

Useful Sites

Analytics and measuring results	Klout, Kred, Google PageSpeed, Wooranks, Cyfy, Google Reader, Pinerly, Statigram, IceRocket
Blog hosting sites	WordPress, Blogger
Blog guests	myblogguest
Dedicated contact sites	Zoom, Teams, Meetup, Eventbrite, Groupspaces, MEETin.org, Citysocializer, Join.me, Google Hangouts, Facetime and Viber
E-tailers	Ebay, Amazon, Etsy, Facebook Market
Feedback/review Sites	TripAdvisor, Google Pages Google Alerts – To track your name
Free training courses	Coursera, Skillshare, Future Learn, Ucademy and LinkedIn learning
Freelancers	upwork.com, guru.com, worksome.com, fiverr.com, truelancer.com, peopleperhour.com, reedsey.com, mypocketskill
General Security	Passwords - howsecureismypassword.com Ad blocker – Ghostery Finding obsolete accounts – accountkiller
Image compressing	JPEG Optimizer, Kraken, TinyPNG, Imagecompressor, Ezgif
Images for free	Pixabay, Unsplash, Canva
Job site	Glassdoor
Keyword search tools	Keyword Surfer, AnswerThePublic, Keyword Sheeter, Keyworddit
Keyword search tools	Keyword Surfer, AnswerThePublic, Keyword Sheeter, Keyworddit
Mobile Wallets	Apple Pay, Samsung Pay, and Google Pay

100 + Top Tips For Social Media Success

Payment gateways	PayPal, Shopify, Stripe
Photo editing and colour testing tools	Animoto, Giphy Gifmaker, Pxlr, Canva, WAVE, Colororacle
Podcast hosting	Buzzsprout, Podbean, Captivate, Transistor, Castos, Spotify, SoundCloud, Pocket Casts, and Stitcher
Podcast hosting sites	thepodcasthost.com
Podcasting tools and advice	Audacity, Garageband, Alitu, thepodcasthost
Print suppliers	Moo, Vistaprint, Instaprint
Professional vlogging	Vimeo
Scheduling sites	Tweetdeck.com, Hootsuite.com, Mailchimp, Buffer.com, Automate SMS messages – Tasker, AutoSMS
Search engines	Google, Microsoft Edge, DuckDuckGo (for added privacy), Safari
SEO	Yoast
Social Media Platforms	LinkedIn, Facebook (Meta), Twitter, Instagram, Pinterest, TikTok, YouTube, Snapchat
Social media information and news	Socialmediaexaminer
Social media tools	Buffer, Hootsuite, Oktopost, SproutSocial
Video tools	Teleprompterprolite, Adobe, Wave.video
Weblink Compressing	Bit.ly.com, Shorturl.at, Tinypng.com
Website creation sites	Hubspot
Website hosting sites	Wix, Weebly, Squarespace, Godaddy, Ionis
Website information sites	Socialmediaexaminer Websitebuilderexpert.com
Word cloud generators for free	Monkeylearn.com, Wordclouds.co.uk Freewordcloudgenerator.com

Government Advice

UK copyright	www.gov.uk/copyright
International copyright	Intellectual Property Office (IPO) Information Centre
Register your logo	Intellectual Property Office (IPO)
Cookie usage	Privacy and Electronic Communications (EC Directive) Regulations 2003
Customer communications	The Electronic Commerce (EC Directive) Regulations 2002
Customer rights	The Consumer Protection (Distance Selling) Regulations 2000 (Business to Consumer)
Data use	The Data Protection Act 2018 is the UK's implementation of the General Data Protection Regulation (GDPR), UK GDPR
Domain name legal registration information	Internet Corporation for Assigned Names and Numbers (ICANN), Nominet (UK)
Accessibility standards	The World Wide Web Consortium (W3C) produces Web Content Accessibility Guidelines (WCAG)

SUMMARY

We hope that you will have found this book of real benefit.

As stated in the Introduction this is one of the first clear guides about how to understand the issues around Social Media and Social Networking in plain English with pragmatic tips.

We continue to play a key part in helping people and organisations to;

- Assess what they need from social media.
- Understand how to develop their strategy/plan.
- Learn how to effectively market on social media.
- Run successful social networking campaigns.

We mentioned before that feedback from clients and readers helps us to further fine tune our material, so please keep the emails coming to; socialnetworking@100toptips.com .

Our best wishes to you all.

Maggie Davies   Sue Smith

THIS FINAL PAGE IS FOR ANY NOTES

Here is a final tip> If you lend this book to someone, put their name and date you lent it on this page. Also add it to your Calendar. This may improve your chance of getting it back!

Lightning Source UK Ltd.
Milton Keynes UK
UKHW050020240522
403422UK00011B/193